LIFTING THE VEIL

LIFTING THE VEIL

by
Debbie Loring

Published by

begin-a-book Independent Publishers
www.beginabook.com

Copyright© 2025 by Debbie Amal Loring

All rights reserved.

No portion of this book may be reproduced in any form without written permission from the publisher or author, except as permitted by UK Copyright Law.

This publication is designed to provide accurate and authoritative information in regard to the subject matter covered. It is sold with the understanding that neither the author nor the publisher is engaged in rendering legal, investment, accounting or other professional services. While the publisher and author have used their best efforts in preparing this book, they make no representations or warranties with respect to the accuracy or completeness of the contents of this book and specifically disclaim any implied warranties of merchantability or fitness for a particular purpose. No warranty may be created or extended by sales representatives or written sales materials. The advice and strategies contained herein may not be suitable for your situation. You should consult with a professional when appropriate. Neither the publisher nor the author shall be liable for any loss of profit or any other commercial damages, including but not limited to special, incidental, consequential, personal, or other damages.

Book Cover by AnnMarie Reynolds for begin-a-book Independent Publishers

Illustrations and Image Content AI generated

First Edition Published in the United Kingdom May 2025

ISBN (Print Edition) 978-1-915353-34-4

ISBN (Digital Edition) 978-1-915353-35-1

Disclaimer Notice

A note about this book and its contents:

Everything contained within these pages is based on my own personal experiences, research, knowledge, viewpoint and understanding. I place no responsibility on any persons involved in this journey for the circumstances and events which comprise my story.

Though I mention Dubai, I state only facts and have sought to represent it and my life there in an entirely factual capacity. The chapters in which I recount events from my time in Dubai are based on my recollections as a Western woman who was raised in a Western culture. My interpretation of these events, therefore, is based on a reference point that differs greatly from the cultural experience and lives of those with whom I was lucky enough to connect. I therefore do not suggest that my observations are correct, nor do I suggest any wrongdoing on the part of any persons I made contact with during my time living in Dubai. I retain the utmost respect for what was once my adopted home and am grateful for the love, care and opportunities provided for both my daughter and myself.

It is important to note that no reference to any persons within my life is intended. My purpose for writing this book is as a platform for exploration of the expectations and restrictions we place upon ourselves. This is the telling of my story and, though it is based loosely on fact, I use it only as a medium to empower and support. In some parts I have added to or detracted from certain circumstances in order to meet this premise. Moreover, my words are not intended to, nor will I ever intend to cause hurt, trauma, negativity or recriminations.

To reiterate: this is my story told in **my own words** based on **my experiences. Any similarities which may seem to relate to existing persons, events, circumstances or situations, are of pure coincidence.**

The only blame for the difficulties I have faced, is placed upon myself.

Debbie x

"I would like to extend my sincere thanks to AnnMarie Reynolds who exercised a great deal of patience with me when writing this book, explaining step by step the whys and hows.

AnnMarie is a wonderful book coach and I couldn't have completed this without her."

AnnMarie can be contacted via *www.beginabook.com / info@beginabook.com*.

Dedicated to my daughter, Kitty.

You are the most amazing, fabulous, talented, kind and generous young woman.

Contents

Chapter One ~ December 2010	11
Chapter Two ~ Present Day	13
Chapter Three ~ How It All Began	19
Chapter Four ~ Spirit - My First Encounter	23
Chapter Five ~ Intuition	27
Chapter Six ~ Patience & Tolerance	31
Chapter Seven ~ November 2004	37
Chapter Eight ~ Starting Over	45
Chapter Nine ~ Managing Change	51
Chapter Ten ~ A Different World	57
Chapter Eleven ~ Learning To Listen	63
Chapter Twelve ~ Learning To Live With Pain	69
Chapter Thirteen ~ Deserving More	85
Chapter Fourteen ~ Struggling On	89
Chapter Fifteen ~ Women & Power	95
Chapter Sixteen ~ On Reflection	101
Chapter Seventeen ~ Coming Home	109
Chapter Eighteen ~ Live For Today	113
Chapter Nineteen ~ Learning Patience	121
Chapter Twenty ~ Discoveries	125
Chapter Twenty One ~ The Next Chapter	129
Chapter Twenty Two ~ Exploring YOU	133
Chapter Twenty Three ~ Final Insights & Wisdom	143
About the Author	149

- 1 -

December 2010

I am driving home from my office, having seen a rather depressed Yemeni client contemplating a second marriage. It is a sunny day in Dubai, December 25th, 2010. When I get home, I will be alone. My daughter, Kitty, is with her father (my first husband), and my current husband is with his other family, flying to Turkey.

Yes, you did read that correctly. My current husband is with his other family.

My mind drifts back to the UK and Christmas, to my mother, brother Barrie, and his wife. Who would have thought I would be as I am today? I am a woman living a different life and culture, far removed from my beginnings in the UK.

Believe it or not, the new tissue box in our bedroom prompted these reflections. The conversation my husband and I had concerning this new tissue box solidified the differences between the woman I once was and the wife I had now become.

I had decided to purchase two rather bling tissue boxes: one for his side of the bed (to replace the existing one) and an identical one for my side. My husband appeared confused, enquiring why I had bought one for myself when I had seemed happy for the previous two years simply using the one on his side of the bed. It was so trivial yet so significant.

"I am becoming more independent," I said. "I don't want to bother you every time I need a tissue."

He'd given me a long look before responding. "You may be more independent in your thinking," he'd replied, "yet you are not more independent. You remain dependent on me."

I said nothing further and acquiesced as I so often did.

This conversation was not out of the ordinary. When I married my second husband, I was fascinated by his religion. I liked the name Amal (which means 'hope' in Arabic), so I added this name to my birth name, Debbie, to embrace my new marriage and identity. I also learned to obey my husband simply because that was the expectation placed upon women of the culture I was now immersed in. I had come a long way from the old Debbie who, living in the UK, would have reacted badly to being told she was 'dependent on another person'. The old Debbie was the polar opposite - fiercely independent and didn't need or want to rely on anyone other than herself – so the mere suggestion of being 'dependent' on someone else would have given rise to anger and a sarcastic retort. The old Debbie would have ensured the person addressing her knew she meant business.

Debbie Amal, though, was different.

By December 2010, I was Debbie Amal, and as such, I simply agreed.

- 2 -

Present Day

My story, though complex, weaves a cautionary tale, a tale which I have finally decided to share. Through my eyes, I want to allow you a glimpse into another world, another life, another time, because I am, and have been, two very different people, each with their own values and beliefs.

After a journey of two halves, two worlds even, I am now back in my land of birth and, with the luxury of reflection, am ready to tell my story—not to name, shame, or blame, for I will do none of these.

My intention is to empower. As you read my story, I want you to bear one thing in mind, for it is this which drives me to share what has, at times, been incredibly painful. Remember this:

> *I am an ordinary woman, like every other woman in this world. If you identify with even a fraction of my story, then bear this in mind: I survived, and so can you.*

If I can do this, so can you. That is a promise.

Learning to be a Single Mother

About a year after my daughter was born in September 2001, my first husband and I started trying for another baby. During this time, I had three miscarriages and considered every possible method to help conceive. Ovulation sticks, moon cycles, crystals, psychics, you name it, I tried it, with no success. Eventually, we resorted to IVF. We had three rounds, which were also unsuccessful, so by now I was broken and destroyed.

It was an incredibly difficult period of my life, made worse by the fact that everyone around me seemed to be pregnant. Of course they weren't, it's just that my mind was in such a vulnerable state that I ended up focusing on pregnant women, which made it seem as if they were everywhere.

My story in this regard is not unremarkable. Sadly, there are thousands of women in the same situation, some of whom are not even fortunate enough to give birth to one child, so through my heartache, I was able to experience gratitude for Kitty, the beautiful daughter who had blessed my world.

The reason for sharing this time in my life is because I eventually came to the realisation that I was only ever meant to have one child. Spirit (in the form of my mentor, John – more later) assured me that this was my destiny and that my husband didn't want another child. He (my husband) was simply going along with the process to appease me. I didn't believe John. How could this be true? My husband wanted a sibling for Kitty just as much as I did, yet the nagging feeling persisted.

One day, having resigned myself to the fact that I was not meant to birth another child, I worked up the courage to ask my husband if he'd ever really wanted another baby. His response cut deep.

"No," he'd said, "Kitty is enough."

He'd then gone on to explain how he was sick of being second best (in my world) to Kitty, and to have another child would have moved him even further down the chain of attention.

To say I was shocked was an understatement. I fervently believed I gave as much to my husband as I possibly could and failed to see how having another baby would result in such a negative impact on him. I was also confused at what appeared to me to be an incredibly selfish attitude. I couldn't understand how any parent would put their own needs ahead of their child(ren). I was to realise later that this was indeed his nature.

Although it was hard to hear and painful at the time, I now realise that this was the reason I wasn't blessed with a sibling for Kitty. Spirit understood that another child would only bring more heartache, so having Kitty and Kitty alone had been my chosen path. This was reaffirmed years later when my first marriage ended and I became a single mother.

My decisions, when it was just Kitty and I, led me to places I could never have imagined, to an existence that became the complete opposite of what I had left behind. I was endlessly searching, and only now, as I sit and write, do I begin to understand the fruitlessness of this search.

Why do I say fruitless?

Because I already had everything I needed. All the answers to life's challenges were within me - I just needed to discover their existence and then learn how to access them.

What I am referring to here is wisdom, which we learn with experience and mistakes. These are not things we are born knowing; they are formed from a complex web of insecurity and life's learning. The story I am about to share is not revealed within these pages for vanity's sake; no, it is told in the hope of supporting, empowering or even inspiring others who may find themselves on a similar path.

As 2025 has just begun, I feel that the time is right for me to open my world and use my story to provide reassurance that you are not alone.

Though I have an incredible connection with the Spirit world, I don't consider myself anything other than ordinary. Looking back at my life, I am surprised at the extent of change I have undergone. Sometimes, I cannot believe the decisions and compromises I have made. My life has been unusual, perhaps even extraordinary, yet in my core and soul I am a Spiritual being, living a human existence and learning what it is to *be* human.

As such, I am the same as every other person on this planet.

The Endless Cycle of Fear and Worry

I have the same fears, worries, and day-to-day struggles as you. My life has been heaven, and it has been hell. There have been countless times when I doubted I would get through each day, yet I did. Somehow, I found the strength deep within to take the next step and make a change. These changes (though they also benefited me) were, most importantly, changes I *had* to make for my daughter.

I tell you my story as a matter of fact, without false pretence or belief that my worth is above others. And I tell it not in consideration of me being special in any way. I will relay my story exactly as it happened because that is the truth. Everything you are about to read has been my reality, and the *most important message is that I survived.*

The journey I share is less about the *who* and the *why* and more about *how*. How I went from being a 'typical' married mother, birthing and raising her daughter as an expat, to a life of discipline and submission in a culture far removed from everything I had ever known.

It was a profound moment when I finally realised that my search for answers was fruitless and that I already had everything I needed within me. Though that realisation has been gradual, I have now reached a point of 'completeness' if you like, and it is from here that I reassure you.

If I, a self-proclaimed ordinary woman, can survive this life journey with all its twists and turns, then so can you.

Whatever your road, whatever your story, whatever picture you wish to paint for your future, all you have to *remember* is that *you can*.

Read my story, hear my words, and learn the lessons I was forced to along the way. I can't guarantee that your passage will be easy, yet what I *can* guarantee you is this: **you are your own destiny–no one else gets to choose.**

I speak from experience. This may be the hardest lesson of all to learn, yet when I finally understood this, that was the exact moment I became free.

Remember, therefore, my simple message, which you will find me repeating often.

If I can do it, so can you.

You have it inside of you in the same way that I did, and really, that's all you need to know.

- 3 -

How It All Began

My start in life was initially unremarkable. I was born to an average family, the youngest child of three and the only girl. My eldest brother was eight years old when I was born, and he, along with my other brother (who definitely has 'middle child syndrome'), had little use for a baby sister. Some of my earliest memories are of loneliness, feeling left out, and perhaps even abandonment. As adults, our sibling relationship has been difficult, to the extent that I have not spoken to my middle brother since 1996. This has not been my choice. I have made several attempts over the years, yet I have been rebuffed and told in no uncertain terms to 'go away'. My brother holds very deep-seated anger issues, and I have recently learned that I am not the only person he's cut ties with. I often think of the old saying, *'blood is thicker than water'*, and wonder at its validity, for it has certainly not been true of my family.

Shortly after I was born, my father was diagnosed with MS (multiple sclerosis). Back then, it was not as well understood as it is today, and I believe my mother struggled to cope with three young children and a sick husband.

I wasn't very old when my father was sent to a hospital in London - referred to as a 'home for the incurables' – and though I was only just old enough to start school, I knew instinctively that my father would not be returning. In the end, he went on to live for a further thirteen years, yet I had been right.

He never did come home.

Living with my Grandmother

Around the same time my father went into the hospital, I was sent to live with my grandmother, even though my brothers remained with Valerie (my mother—she disliked being called mother). I was told this was because my mother needed to work and couldn't look after me, whereas my brothers, who were that bit older, could better fend for themselves.

Growing up with my grandmother was an experience I will forever cherish. She was the polar opposite of my mother who could be challenging to be around. Valerie feared everything and embedded that fear in us children, too.

My mother would say things like, *"Don't take risks, stick with what you know, there are more bad times than good, don't try anything new, don't travel, don't try new foods,"* which made navigating life as a young girl and then teenager very difficult. I found it hard to know what I could believe or hold onto. How should I react or respond? I guess it was only natural then that I turned inward for answers.

My grandmother, as I said, was the complete opposite. She was a kind, gentle, and patient lady who even took early retirement to be there for me. I remember visiting my father in the hospital, though not in any detail. The only real memory I have is when my mother took us to visit him for the last time – I had been around five years old. It was not a happy visit. My mother became angry with my father, though I don't know why. He had begun getting confused by this stage, so perhaps that fuelled Valerie's frustration because right there, in the 'home for the incurables', she demanded a divorce.

My father's mental capacity was compromised by then, and he lacked the ability to consent to her demand. Valerie's parting shot, therefore, was full of vitriol.

"I wish you would die," she shouted to my father. "I wish you would die so that I could be free."

The Passing of my Parents

I never saw my father again – not only that, we were also forbidden from talking about him, and sadly, he played no part in my upbringing. Reflecting now, as an adult, I am sure my parents' marriage had been fraught with difficulty and perhaps the way my mother behaved towards us was her way of coping.

On the day my father died, Valerie muttered only two words: good riddance.

My mother passed away in September 2011. She'd had cancer. When I heard about her illness, I wanted to return home (back to the UK), yet she discouraged me from doing so. It *"wasn't what she wanted"*, she'd said.

I can reflect on her life now and see that perhaps it didn't unfold as she wished, which is sad. She was an intelligent, attractive lady, yet her negativity about everything made her difficult to be around at times.

As a mother, she was quick to reprimand and hesitant to praise, which influenced how others reacted to her. This only intensified her negativity.

We held a humanist funeral for her, and my second husband travelled from Dubai to attend. It was an unusual occasion, representing a rather unremarkable conclusion to the life of a woman who, had her journey taken a different route, might have found much happiness. Although I didn't realise it at the time, this marked the beginning of the end of my second marriage.

- 4 -

Spirit ~ My First Encounter

Throughout this story, I will refer to my relationship with the Spirit world. Though it can be difficult to explain, I will endeavour to share stories and experiences as they become relevant.

I remember my very first Spiritual encounter as if it were yesterday, though I was still a child, only eight years of age. I was with my grandmother and mother. We had been to visit some friends in Theale, Berkshire, England and were on our way home when the fan belt on my mother's car broke. Cars back then were much less complicated than they are today, so it was often the case that we would be resourceful in temporarily mending such problems. A broken fan belt was routinely replaced by a pair of stockings until a proper repair could be undertaken. On this occasion, the stockings my grandmother removed from her person and fixed in place of the fan belt did not work, which meant we were stuck until the car could be fixed the following day. Only then would we be able to make our way home.

Fortunately, we had friends nearby who were happy to accommodate us overnight. The lady had a dog named Bobby, and in the middle of the night, I woke up and went downstairs to get a glass of water, accompanied by Bobby. Suddenly, my attention was drawn to the sound of piano music, so I went into the living room to find out who was awake and playing the piano at this late hour. When I arrived, I saw a woman I didn't recognise sitting on the piano stool, her fingers flying over the keys. She heard me approach and turned around.

'Hello,' she said.

I moved closer to listen; oddly, Bobby refused to enter the room. After a few moments, the lady stopped playing, got up from the stool, and walked straight through the wall into the house next door. I had no idea what to think, yet despite the strangeness of this encounter, I knew with certainty that I wasn't scared.

When I retold my story the following day, I referred to the piano-playing lady as a ghost, for in my mind, that is what she had been. Valerie responded, telling me I was being silly and to stop making up stories.

"There are no ghosts," she'd said - and that had been the end of that.

Later, I asked the woman we were staying with who the lady was. To my surprise, our host looked visibly shocked. She told me that it could only have been her sister who died twenty years earlier. The sister's bedroom was on the other side of the wall she had exited through because when she was alive, the house was one large property with no wall between. After finishing her piano playing last night, she had simply returned to her bedroom.

I knew what I had seen and how reluctant Bobby had been to enter the room with me, so after hearing about the sister who had passed away, I knew that my mother was wrong and that what I had experienced was real.

By the time I'd reached the age of sixteen, Valerie's influence had begun to take hold over me, though it wasn't until many years later that I understood this. Sixteen saw me starting to rebel and change my appearance. I felt as if something inside of me had snapped. The first to go was my long red hair, which had always fallen to the base of my spine. I chopped it off in favour of a skinhead before methodically cutting up my school uniforms and stitching them back together with safety pins.

It's fair to say that I fully embraced the punk era, and with that came nightclubs, dancing and boys – though this is where I was different to my friends.

My best friend Marion and I would go out clubbing, and though there were male advances, I rebuffed these, opting to enjoy the music and dancing without any contact from the opposite sex. It didn't occur to me at the time to question this – it was how I felt.

Valerie had always taught me that teenage boys (and men) were only after one thing and that I was not to be labelled as 'that girl'. Reflecting on this, I can see that her influence worked, as I actively avoided many advances during my teenage years. That's not to say she was wrong; I am sure many of those making such advances were driven by hormones and had only one goal in mind. It's just that I was unable to see any alternatives. Thus, I grew up harbouring a particular attitude toward the opposite sex, which was undoubtedly a by-product of my upbringing. The endless cautionary tales were deeply ingrained.

Intuition

You will recall that I had not seen my father since the age of five, so it was somewhat of a surprise when, at the age of fourteen, I experienced an overwhelming urge to visit him in the 'home for the incurables'.

My friend Marcia agreed to accompany me to the nursing home, so we planned our trip to Stretton the following Monday. Given that it had been almost ten years since I last had contact with my father, it was a strange feeling – confusing even – wanting to visit him now after all that time. Yet, I somehow knew it was Spirit pressing me to make contact before my father passed.

On Sunday, the day before our planned trip, my mother told me that the police had come to the house and informed her that my father had died. I didn't know how to feel. My emotions were all over the place. All I knew was that despite my best efforts, I had been unable to get to my father in time.

In the manner I had grown accustomed to, my mother simply reiterated her words from a decade ago.

'Good riddance', she'd said - though my emotions were much more complex. Despite such a lack of parental relationship with my father, the feelings around his death were hard to grasp. Knowing he had gone left me with a weird kind of 'emptiness'.

Valerie's dislike of my father ran deep. If nothing else, I know she resented him for 'leaving her with three millstones around her neck'- my brothers and me. All three of us were under no illusions that we would be sent away as soon as possible, which is how I came to live with my grandmother. Before then, I was often threatened with being sent to the children's home. Although I didn't know exactly what that meant, I do remember being incredibly scared.

On one occasion, my grandmother was on holiday, so I returned to stay with my mother for a while. I think I was about six years old. One of the days I was there, Valerie was in a state about something and walked out of the door, telling me that she was 'going to get in the car and drive into a brick wall and kill myself'. Then she promptly left, and I burst into tears. My eldest brother appeared.

"She says that all the time," he reassured, "she will be back".

My brother was right. Valerie did return, though I can remember the situation and words so vividly. Such was their lasting effect.

Proof of Spirit and Three Stages of Intuition

This message telling me to visit my father was further proof (not that I needed it) of the Spirit's presence in my life. As I've matured, changed careers, moved to a different country, become a wife and mother, etc., one thing that has remained constant is my connection with the Spirit world, which manifests in so many ways today.

I have learned to listen to my *intuition* because I recognise **this as my inner guidance**.

In fact, I believe it is the inner guidance for us all, regardless of which theory of survival we subscribe to.

For me, the key to intuition is not to over-think it—simply sit with it and listen to what it says. From bitter experience, I can say with a hand on my heart that when I have chosen to ignore my intuition, the results have been less than positive—sometimes even catastrophic.

Intuition, as I have come to learn, has *three stages*. For simplicity, I will explain how it works when I meet someone (for the first time).

Stage One:

Let's say I have just met John and am deciding if I like him.
My first instinct may be that, no, I don't like him.
Equally, my first instinct could be that I do like John.

Stage Two:

In the middle of the two choices, between liking and disliking John, lies a grey area where I am 'not sure' about my feelings toward him. This is the moment when we need to pause and reflect on our intuition, allowing the natural course of events to unfold.

While we will come to know John during this stage, we cannot compel ourselves into either a 'like' or 'dislike' mindset – even if we wanted to.

Stage Three:

To make the right choice, we must be patient. We should allow our relationships with others to develop at their own pace. To achieve this, I trust my intuition and practice ***patience*** and ***tolerance***. Then I wait.

I wait for my intuition to decide. I wait for proof of that person's actions to support my current position. I wait for messages from Spirit, and I allow every element to unfold at the right time.

This is what I mean about Spirit and intuition, and it is something we can all tap into with relative ease if we start practising those two basic values of *patience* and *tolerance*.

- 6 -

Patience and Tolerance

You might wonder why I am sharing this now, and I understand your confusion. We've gone from my father's passing when I was fourteen and the promise of my story being told to ***patience*, *tolerance,* and *intuition***, so you would be right to wonder where I am going with this and what it has to do with you.

Though it might not be apparent why right now, I want you to remember these values—***patience*** and ***tolerance***—and hold them in your heart as you read the rest of my story.

I also want you to consider how they apply to your everyday life and see if you can exercise more ***patience*** and ***tolerance*** as you navigate each day. One way to achieve this is by objectively assessing which elements of your life and daily existence you *can* control and which you *cannot*. Once you understand how little control you likely have over most of the areas that trouble you, you will find a certain amount of peace. If you don't control it, you cannot change it. It's as simple as that.

A dear friend and mentor imparted the most important life lesson I have ever received. A lesson so beautiful in its simplicity yet so appropriate to every single one of us. Though this wonderful mentor has passed on, he remains by my side, Spiritually guiding me. He is always there whenever I need him. He is the one presence I know will never let me down:

When we find ourselves in a situation where we feel forced to react – we always do the opposite of what is desired.

Consider this for a moment. When we are forced to *react* to a situation – perhaps when we feel backed into a corner and must make a split-second decision – we usually resort to fighting. However, fighting is not the desired outcome. If we engage in fighting, we will not resolve anything; rather, we will likely escalate upset and provoke antagonistic behaviour in others. Therefore, we must learn to *respond rather than react*, as *responding* fosters positive emotions with controllable outcomes, whilst *reacting* tends to cultivate negative emotions with results that are unlikely to be constructive.

It's human nature. ***When backed into a corner, we fight. Instead, we should learn how to respond*** so that, eventually, we can overcome our inbuilt need to ***react (negatively)***.

This is an important point. As you are focusing on ***patience*** and ***tolerance***, focus also on the difference between ***reacting*** to a situation and ***responding*** to the same situation. If we ***react***, chances are that will produce a ***negative outcome***, yet if we ***respond***, it is likely that the outcome will be positive. Why? Because to ***respond*** means to have taken time to consider, to think, to work out how to give the most beneficial answer, whereas to ***react*** is instinctive and is often driven by negative emotions such as anger or mistrust. This is covered in more detail in the next chapter.

John and Jeanette

John was a Spiritual minister trained by the Spiritual National Union (SNU), the largest organisation of its kind in the UK. A mutual friend introduced me to John and his partner, Jeanette, at a bonfire night in Ripley, Surrey. I immediately liked John, although my connection with Jeanette took longer. Initially, I felt that Jeanette was a bit too feminine and girly for me (remember the punk?!).

There was a fun fair at the bonfire, so Jeanette and I tried our hand at the firing range, shooting down a few targets until I eventually won a little red devil stuffed toy. Very fitting!

From the get-go, John had a presence about him. He was calm, and his belief in Spirit was unquestioned. In fact, his mother was a very well-known medium.

John and Jeanette travelled all over the country and, indeed, worldwide, comforting people with messages of hope and proof of survival. Their message was simple. They wanted to show as many people as they could this:

That we live beyond the physical death of our bodies.

Unlike many mediums you see now, John wasn't about appearances. There was no showmanship involved. He simply worked with people from all walks of life and brought them hope by showing them that love continues. It was his mission to prove to those he encountered that his message was true. That we do live beyond our physical death.

Both John and Jeanette were very accurate mediums. They readily provided details of those who had passed - confirming that we survive beyond our physical form. I spent many hours on the phone from Dubai to John, who lived in Surrey, which resulted in high telephone bills, yet that didn't stop me - I always had so much to ask.

From a young age, I'd been curious about the Spiritual world, yet I wanted proof—something definitive that would allow me to 'let go' and 'believe'. I distinctly remember one day when John told me to go into the bathroom, look in the mirror, and then look over my right shoulder.

"Okay," I'd replied, "I'll call you back."

I did exactly what he said, I looked into the mirror, then turned my head over my right shoulder. I was amazed when I saw the most beautiful 'being' of light, formed in the shape of a Russian doll (or something similar). It had the most beautiful purple auric field with a white centre. I was so surprised that I turned completely around to look, but the image had disappeared.

John explained that what I had witnessed was seen through my third eye and wasn't something my 'physical' eyes could see. He asked if that was proof enough.

John passed away in 2007; Jeanette survives him. She remains one of my closest confidantes and is always an inspiration. We reflect on John often, recalling the wisdom he shared, including those three elements I introduced a moment ago.

It is thanks to John that I realised I needed to:

- Learn to respond, *not* react
- Learn to be patient
- Learn to become tolerant

In 1998, John and Jeanette visited me in Dubai, and we held a meditation circle, which was attended by over 50 people. He was always incredibly kind and understanding whenever he was asked for 'proof', which I saw him give repeatedly. John had time for everyone, and I am so incredibly fortunate that I still get to hear his wisdom and feel his calming presence as he visits me in my times of need.

When John first encouraged me not to **react**, he discussed how we often **rush in** and **react** without thinking things through - a typical 'knee-jerk reaction'. The problem with this approach is that we don't give ourselves the space to form an appropriate response. Our initial reaction might be fine, even spot on, yet if we don't take a moment to pause, we risk overreacting or even catastrophising, which increases our stress levels. Additionally, we may unintentionally offend others, emphasising the importance of *understanding the difference between reacting and responding*.

The difference between **Reacting** and **Responding**

"It is," John told me, "All about your breath. When faced with a situation that requires a reaction, allow yourself a moment to take a deep breath in and then breathe slowly out. Repeat this for a few seconds, giving your brain time to assimilate, digest and create the most appropriate response."

My grandmother was a firm believer in this approach.

"Take a breath and count to twenty," she would say.

If you do this often enough, it will become a habit, and you'll soon realise it's the perfect way to create a space or gap in the situation. This gap will then enable you to *respond* rather than *react*. That being said, it's far from easy. We are all so busy trying to fill every moment of our lives with meaning, activities, and purpose that taking a few seconds to breathe each time we feel ourselves slipping into a negative reactive state can feel counterproductive.

One way to overcome this feeling of 'counterproductive-ness' is to focus on the two values of ***patience*** and ***tolerance***. Regardless of how effective your quest to *respond* rather than *react* is, if you can focus on becoming more *patient* and *tolerant*, you will still see a positive difference in your interactions with others. That alone will lead to a more measured and less stressful solution.

Even though we haven't reached my story yet, and I haven't fully illustrated how all of this fits in, you can still start working on ***responding*** rather than ***reacting***. Incorporate these words into your daily life alongside ***patience*** and ***tolerance,*** and strive to improve your ability to *react*. Personally, this simple change has felt empowering and helped me stay strong during times of true adversity. It has also aided me in understanding who I am, what I want, *and* what I deserve.

Why not take a moment to do it now? Slow down, allow yourself the breathing space to make conscious choices—perhaps around a stressful situation—and see if you can choose to respond rather than react. I promise you won't regret it, and it will put you in the perfect frame of mind to align your emotions and challenges with those I have been forced to explore as part of my journey.

My desire is for you to take what you need from my story. It and this book are not blueprints for your future, nor are they a plan or even a how-to guide. I am simply one (flawed) human being sharing my journey with a single goal in mind:

To help those who are struggling at any level in life learn how to survive, whatever the situation.

I want you to take strength from the knowledge that if someone like me can get through the story you are about to read, then you can absolutely make it through your journey, too.

That's not to say it will be easy, so take the time to listen to your ***intuition***, breathe, slow down, and try to eliminate anything other than a ***response*** (not a ***reaction***). Ultimately, I know you will find an outcome that delivers exactly what you need.

- 7 -

November 2004

<u>The Beginning of the End</u>

Let's go back in time – albeit metaphorically.

Wouldn't it be great to correct what we believe we have done wrong and soothe the pain we have caused? Yet, time travel isn't possible—at least not as far as we know. Instead, we need to use the tools available to us and allow them to help us navigate our future.

Many of us have yet to realise that we possess far more knowledge and insight than we recognise. One of the most powerful tools readily at our disposal is, as I've mentioned before, our intuition. This can significantly aid us in becoming the best version of ourselves. Hopefully, you're starting to understand that your intuition is incredibly important!

It's true that we cannot right our wrongs by erasing them; we can, though, reflect on our past and take the learnings from this reflection forward.

For the purposes of my story, I want to go back to November 2004.

My childhood was far from straightforward, so it is unsurprising that I followed some of those same difficult paths when it came to my own life and relationships. By November 2004, my first husband and I had been married for five years, and we had our beautiful daughter, Kitty, who was three years old. I thought everything was going well.

What I Wanted, Not What I Needed

Looking back, there were several red flags that I wilfully ignored when I met my first husband in 1999. As our relationship progressed to marriage, I naively thought he ticked enough boxes to be my forever future. Now, many years later, I can see that I was looking for him to be what *I thought I wanted* rather than what *I actually needed*.

We met at a party, and on first encounter, he had all the attributes I wanted—his own house, well-travelled, liked good food, was self-sufficient and fun to be around. I had been on my own for a long time with a successful career, yet my existence was materialistic. Though I had everything money could buy, I wasn't happy. My first husband seemed to be the final piece of the puzzle.

In the early days of our relationship, I ignored a huge red flag. On one of our first dates, we went to a local pub, where we chatted and shared stories, spending a pleasant afternoon getting to know each other. During this conversation, he told me that I 'wasn't his usual type.'

"Normally, I go out with girls who are more facially attractive than you," he'd said, "though I am prepared to make an exception."

Shocked, I muttered an expletive and immediately walked out, only to return when he promptly burst into tears and begged forgiveness. The nurturer in me kicked in, and I forgave him. Despite more similar comments (asking the girl on the makeup counter in Harrods to 'see what she could do with this', indicating my face), I continued our relationship, even walking down the aisle.

Whenever I reflect on what I could or perhaps should have done differently back then, I remind myself that if it were not for this marriage, I would be without the gift of my daughter. Thus, I have come to understand that my first marriage's 'soul' purpose was to bring my daughter onto this earthly plane.

Not long after we became engaged in 1997, a couple of years before we married, my then-fiancé secured a job in Dubai, and I went with him, excited about the prospect of a fresh start. I sought and found my own employment with relative ease, though, after a couple of years, it became apparent that this role was not fulfilling. The company I worked for had a different moral and ethical compass than mine, which led me, in 1999 (while still residing in Dubai), to take tentative steps toward setting up my first company.

A Happy Marriage

During our marriage, we divided our time between Dubai and Cumbria in the Lake District, England. The property we owned in the UK was a beautiful 18th-century barn that had been converted into a house and was nestled within a sleepy countryside hamlet. We completed the purchase of the house around Christmas 2004, even though we had never intended to buy a property. Initially, we had planned an incredible trip to visit Soneva Gili (a stunning, albeit expensive, island in the Maldives) for the Christmas season, yet as the date drew nearer, a series of mishaps occurred.

First, our accommodation was booked incorrectly, and the flights did not match. The tour operator then continued to make mistake after mistake, and after about three weeks of battling to arrange everything, I gave up and instead turned my focus to purchasing a property in the UK. Since we were splitting our time between Dubai and England, it made sense for us to have a permanent base in the UK.

It didn't take long for us to find a house that we loved, yet, in line with the streak of bad luck I was experiencing in 2004, the solicitor made an oversight, which meant we lost that property. The 18th-century barn conversion we eventually bought was offered as a 'consolation' alternative to the house we'd set our hearts on - though I fell in love with it as soon as I saw it. It had everything I'd ever wanted. In little more than six weeks, it was ours.

By a strange coincidence, the barn's previous owner was a retired gentleman who spent a lot of time in Qatar, which is only an hour's flight from Dubai. He and his wife had left the house spotless, along with a fair few Arabic rugs for us to enjoy.

A few weeks later, I watched in horror as the tsunami in Asia brought devastation and suffering beyond comprehension. One of the islands affected was Soneva Gili, which, except for the grace of divine intervention, is where I, my first husband, and my daughter would have been. With all those thousands of lives lost and the utter desolation in its wake, I recall taking a moment of quiet reflection to look around our quaint, cosy cottage and feeling immensely grateful.

An Unhappy Marriage

Despite the happiness we found in our home, by 2004 it became apparent that our marriage was not as strong as I'd once thought. My husband had confessed to 'paying' for certain pleasures, and there was absolutely no doubt his now closest friend could be found at the bottom of a bottle.

His defence (to this cheating) consisted of a blow-by-blow account of precisely what happened and the comment that he was *'lonely when I was back in the UK'*. I was deeply hurt. The marriage had been fine until he'd started paying for sex. Regardless, I maintained the pretence. I didn't know what else to do; honestly, all I cared about was protecting our beautiful daughter.

Our strained arrangement continued. We lived in Dubai and returned to the UK for holidays when it became too hot to stay in Dubai. These holidays usually lasted a couple of months, during July and August, which is what passes for a UK summer. Three years after I learned of my husband's extra-marital activities, we arrived in August 2007, and I was completely fed up. The constant rain and lack of sunshine, though a welcome relief from the punishing Dubai heat, had started to get to me, and I began to feel trapped.

I love the Lake District, yet even there, amongst all its natural beauty, I craved space. I wanted freedom and escape.

From what?

I didn't know.

Escaping

My need for a break became all-consuming. When my husband returned from Dubai and was due to stay in the UK for a while, I decided to swap places with him. Kitty was five years old, so he and our daughter finished their holiday in the UK whilst I returned to our home in Dubai alone. They would both then join me a few weeks later.

The need to be in Dubai came from my intuition, which was telling me that I could work hard there and build my business by expanding my network. My intuition told me this was the key to the freedom and happiness I craved, and as I travelled alone, ahead of my husband and daughter, I experienced a sense of excitement that had been missing for a very long time.

During the times when my husband and I were both abroad, we would rent out our beautiful cottage for holidaymakers. The practice beforehand was to clean the house from top to bottom and pack everything away in cupboards, which was usually my job. In 2007, that task fell to my husband since I had already left for Dubai, though neither of us could have known that in 2007, as my husband packed up our beautiful barn home, it would be the last time either of us would undertake to do so.

I was not concerned about leaving my husband and Kitty behind. I knew they would be joining me in a couple of weeks, and I looked forward to having some space and time to myself. Things in our marriage hadn't been the same for me since he admitted to sleeping with a prostitute – unprotected! – and I was struggling with my feelings, especially since his social dependency on alcohol was becoming increasingly obvious and, though vanity was not part of this discourse, my husband's waistline was ever-expanding. I could barely believe he'd tried to convince me that his indiscretion was solely due to being lonely when we were apart.

I boarded the plane with no hand luggage except a copy of the Qur'an that I had bought from a bookshop in Windermere. I had always been interested in the religion of the country where I worked and lived, so I figured reading the Qur'an would be the perfect way to start immersing myself into that world and culture, and when better to read it than on the outgoing flight?

So, there I was, in August 2007, skinny jeans, LV bag and a tight pink low-cut top, enjoying the flight from Manchester airport to Dubai. I already felt a sense of freedom I hadn't experienced in years. I was sitting in the aisle next to an elderly couple who were on their way to Australia via Dubai. I remember smiling when they told me that Dubai was simply their stop on the way. Nobody visits Dubai in August. Its average temperature of 45 degrees plus makes it far from ideal. I would have been more surprised to hear them say they were planning to remain in Dubai.

In the centre aisle was an Iranian man and his two sons, one of whom couldn't take his eyes off me. What a strange enigma I must have seemed, a Western woman reading a copy of the Qur'an. The religion intrigued me, though. When I first moved to Dubai and heard the Athan (the call to prayer), something stirred in me, and the more I discovered, the more I came to like the structure and logic of Islam. On the plane, I began trying to understand what the Qur'an said about women. I wanted to understand why women were typically suppressed by this religion, which was something I had witnessed during my time in the country.

As we continued our journey, wine was offered with our meal. I declined. Alcohol was something I had chosen to give up a year or so before – though it had not been an easy accomplishment. For me, I found it wasn't so much about actually giving it up; it was about the enormous social pressure I was under to keep drinking in order to stay 'within my group of peers'. I endured constant questions about why I wasn't drinking and cajoling to 'just have one'. I had my reasons for no longer drinking alcohol, and no matter how hard some made it for me to do so, I stood firm. What also became apparent when my visions were not blurred by alcohol was how little I had in common with a lot of the people I spent time with.

There's a historical stereotype of British society – an idea that our lives are based on or revolve around pubs. A British 'tradition' if you like, and to an extent, it is a British institution, yet not to the degree it is sometimes portrayed.

Many outside of the UK are influenced in their understanding of our culture by what they see on television, and it isn't necessarily true that we turn to alcohol in times of need. In fact, there are far fewer pubs in the UK today than there used to be, though it is true that we usually put the kettle on to make a typical English cuppa in times of stress. I digress.

When people don't drink, or rather they have stopped, it is assumed they have a problem with alcohol or that it's a temporary detox – like *Dry January*. As neither of these applied to me, I was made to feel abnormal about my decision to give up 'the booze' and was put under a great deal of pressure to conform with the majority.

After declining wine on the flight to Dubai in 2007, I once more became aware of the young Iranian man seated in the centre row, watching me. When I stood up to stretch and go to the toilet, I took the opportunity to have a closer look. He must have been eighteen at the most, which probably explained why I, in my Western clothing, was proving so much of an enigma to him.

- 8 -

Starting Over

<u>Or so I thought ...</u>

I arrived in Dubai to 48-degree heat. My first thought was, 'Thank God I had arrived,' and my second was that my 'oh so tight jeans' were 'oh so not such a good idea!'

When I reached my home in Dubai, I felt free for the first time in a very long while. I remember dancing like crazy for about four hours, turning up the sound system and burning off energy as I embraced the lightness I felt within.

Reading the Qur'an on the plane intrigued me, and I knew I wanted to learn more. After embracing my freedom by dancing until I had nothing left, I sat down and continued to read, only to awake the following morning knowing that I wanted to explore Islam in more depth; I just wasn't sure how.

The logical place was the nearest shopping mall, though I was unsure what had drawn me there. Then, I spotted the Dubai Tourism Department of Information desk and walked boldly up to the Emirati.

"Do you have any information about Islam?" I asked.

I must have spoken more quietly than intended because he didn't hear me.

"What?" he responded.

The use of the word "what" rather than "pardon" has always irritated me, so I decided to correct him. "You mean pardon?"

"What? What?" he repeated, and it took every ounce of patience I had not to walk away. Instead, I decided to communicate as clearly as possible, speaking slowly to avoid misunderstanding.

"Do you have any information relating to Islam?" I asked.

On this occasion, he heard me, for which I was grateful, though I was embarrassed that I'd had to raise my voice. At that point, I would have preferred to ask him where I could buy haemorrhoid cream!

The question was finally understood, and the man proceeded to rummage around for an eternity until he produced a piece of paper with a telephone number. I was to call a lady at the nearby Islamic Centre. I left reasonably satisfied because at least now, I had a starting point.

A couple of days later, I made the call, and a happy Egyptian woman answered, telling me that the lady I needed to contact was currently away in Egypt and would be back in a couple of weeks – which meant I had to wait.

Disappointed, I determined that I would explore the newfound freedom I had gained from temporarily breaking away from my relationship while waiting for the lady to return from Egypt. I went to the gym, happily working out in the men's section, and treating myself to a Personal Trainer who took great delight in telling me that my body fat was TOO LOW! Wow, I thought, how many women have that?! I also spent time in my favourite nightclub, where I would dance for hours on end, drink water and try to avoid advances from men.

Building A New Life

When I first arrived in Dubai all those years ago, the job I secured had been within a large IT company, yet I was never completely satisfied. Eventually, I came to the realisation that my dissatisfaction related to money and material goods. Not that I wanted more, far from it. I realised that money and material goods did nothing to serve humanity, and I was starting to feel a strong desire to help others.

It took a while, though; finally, the pieces began to fit together. I decided to go to the US to study NLP (Neurolinguistic Psychology), Hypnosis, and Timeline Therapy. Once I qualified, I returned to Dubai and became a counsellor, opening my own clinic in 1999. I was worried about finding clients or even if the right clients were out there, so I placed an advert in a local magazine and hoped for the best.

My concerns were unfounded; I was one of the few qualified hypnotherapists and counsellors in Dubai – which meant plenty of clients and all manner of issues.

As I reflect on those days, I feel that I pretty much saw it all. From rape, incest and murder, to fears and phobias. You name it, I met it in my clinic. In fact, the first client I ever saw was facing a fear which I also shared.

This client had MS, which was the same illness that had taken my father into the 'home for incurables' and later, taken his life. Through my experiences with this disease as a child I had developed a fear of MS, so when faced with this particular client, I realised I first had to work on ***myself*** to overcome ***my*** fear before I could help that client. It was hard going and gave rise to no end of challenges, so I listened to my intuition and employed my passion for helping this client, which enabled me to address my fear and, thus, open my soul and provide the necessary support.

I also had another deeply rooted fear, which had again embedded as a child. I had once listened to an American actor speaking who had throat cancer. In order to treat his cancer, doctors had removed his larynx (voice box), which meant when he spoke he made the most awful sound. As a child, it terrified me; then, as fate often dictates, my second client in my new Dubai practice was someone who had also had his larynx removed and spoke through a mechanical voice box – the exact sound I had heard all those years earlier. This client's throat had been damaged by smoking, and it was for this he came to me – to seek a way to quit smoking. Of course, I wanted to treat him so again, I was forced to overcome my own demon before I could do so.

It is genuinely interesting that my first two clients both brought up fears I had long thought were buried. These situations serve as perfect examples of the messages we receive, and I realised that by trusting my intuition and understanding why I was confronted with these clients and their challenges, I could re-frame my belief system, resulting in a positive outcome for both myself and my clients.

Those experiences taught me the value of uncovering the root of each client's issue within minutes—a process I greatly enjoyed. Fortunately, I found it straightforward, aided by a technique that partly stems from my connection to the Spirit world. Here's how it worked:

A new client would visit. They would fill out the client details form, and then, before we had gone any further, I would ask them to draw a tree on a piece of paper. Next to this tree they were to draw themselves.

I was then able to place my hand over the drawing and 'tune in' to that person. I was (and still am) able to sense what had happened in their life, even down to specific times and incidents, which allowed me to support them in moving away from those issues and discovering what they wanted for themselves. I know that it is Spirit guides helping me to pinpoint the start of someone's issues

For almost every person, this 'want' was a sense of peace in their hearts or lives, whether this meant having three Porsches on the driveway, running water to their door, or learning to let go of the past.

After managing and overcoming my fears with those first two clients, I began working with new individuals from all walks of life and differing socio-economic backgrounds. As my confidence and experience grew, I realised that it didn't matter where people were from or how much or little they had because they all had the most important of things in common: *they all needed help*. They all wanted peace of mind and to be happy.

We Are All the Same

I have seen the extremely wealthy and the extremely average, those who are dying and those who wish to give life, i.e. have a child. I provided my clients with practical tools, hypnosis, the power of visualisation, neurolinguistic programming (or NLP, which is an approach to communication), personal development and psychotherapy - and most of all, I have provided confidence.

Though I have gone off track a little here (we were talking about discovering Islam), I think it's important to continue with this part of my journey because the guidance I was able to give often came back to my connection with the Spirit world, as illustrated by the relative simplicity of the tree exercise.

I cannot (though I wish I could) take credit for this exercise. It was a tool given to me by the late John Hodge (what a man) and his other half, or better half, as she would say, Jeanette, who remains my dearest friend and closest confidant. John was a wonderful man – though he would often irritate me when he gave deep and meaningful answers to my deep and meaningful questions. I would sometimes crave a simple answer, yet these were rare from John, and many times, I was bemused and left wondering what on earth he meant by his response.

John was a very powerful Medium, as is Jeanette. He was a working Medium in that Spiritualist Churches invited him to come and run their service. This also involved connecting with those in Spirit. To clarify, Spiritualists believe that after the body has died, the Spirit (the element that makes us 'here') continues in a different plane of existence, and it is these Spirits which help us - from their position of freedom - when we are in the material world.

John was an endless source of wisdom, and I loved him deeply. Though he died on July 14, 2007 (over fifteen years ago), I don't miss him because he still comes back to visit me, and I speak to him often. He usually shares his normal earthly wisdom of "patience" and "no reaction—learn to respond," so even though he is no longer on the same plane as me, nothing has changed!

- 9 -

Managing Change

When my first husband and I moved to Dubai at the end of the 1990s, I was completely unprepared for the steep cultural learning curve I was about to embark on. Working and living in a country so vastly different from my birthplace was not without its challenges, which were particularly profound when it came to the women of Dubai and how they lived and worked at the end of the 20th Century.

Before moving to Dubai, my career had been in a predominantly male-dominated environment. The IT industry was still a man's domain at that time, so I thought I knew what to expect in a country where women perhaps had less of a voice than they do now. However, I soon realised I was completely naïve. The expectations of women in the Middle East were vastly diverse, and my approach to work, which had stemmed from a different culture, was not always well-received. Lacking the freedoms I took for granted in the UK, I encountered considerable jealousy from local women who had never experienced a Western life.

Their discomfort around me increased the harder I worked and the more successful a career I forged. I was able to become financially independent and had the freedom that some could only dream of, which made it difficult for me to form any close female companionships. Those women had no way of knowing that I was still in a man's world; the only difference was that I had learned how to survive it.

Back in the UK, to become one of the 'boys' was to play the same game as them. The way to do that was to drink more, swear more, beat them to the next promotion, and so on, inadvertently becoming an honorary man. As a Western woman in a Western world, I had it down pat. Yet none of these previously employed strategies was appropriate for my new culture, so I was forced to find new tools. I was able to use my skills in navigating challenging situations and workplaces, which meant I could survive working life in Dubai, albeit with some adjustments.

Though different, the culture in Dubai became incredibly interesting to me. The first time I heard the call to prayer was almost humbling, and I was blown away by how the locals carried themselves. I also adored their clothing and traditional dress. They were gorgeous—men and women alike—and always smelled divine. As I became ever more immersed in my new society, I realised just how much I had previously misunderstood their religion, and perhaps that is another reason why I was drawn to the Qur'an when I returned alone several years later.

Different Rules

Rules, though, were blatantly different for men and women. It frustrated the hell out of me that Arab men were able to walk around wearing lightweight clothing in deference to the 40-plus degree heat, yet their wives – who always walked behind – were required to wear full regalia, including abaya, niqab, gloves and socks. They must have been boiling. To me, it seemed like a form of torture.

For several years I led a typical expat life, not really mixing with Muslims or Arabs. Incredibly, there are around 207 different nationalities in Dubai, which makes it a very culturally diverse country and one in which I didn't need to worry too much about fitting in.

Even though I loved the local music and lifestyle, there were not many ex-pat women working at the same level as me, so becoming close to or making female friends was difficult. I still recall an incident in my early days when I met with a client in Kuwait (a place I loved). I had hired a driver to chauffeur me around and, given that it was about an hour's drive from the city (of Kuwait) to the client (an oil company), I tried to relax amongst all the reckless driving unfolding around me. It should have been a peaceful journey, yet I witnessed so many more risks being taken on the road than back in Dubai. There were countless abandoned cars on what would be the equivalent of our hard shoulder. New cars, not old cars. Brand new cars.

"So many cars wrecked by the oil-rich youth of Kuwait," observed my chauffeur. Their attitude, he told me, was to 'leave the car there and get a new one.'

Being a Woman in Business

On this particular day, it was really hot, and I mean really hot. As soon as I stepped out of the car, it was like stepping into an aircraft engine. Even my hair was hot, although it was dry, unlike the humidity of Dubai, and I immediately poured with perspiration.

When I arrived, I was greeted with a mixture of curiosity and disapproval. This Western woman stood out like a beacon among the mainly white kandoorahs (traditional-style dresses) in her well-fitted suit, high-heeled shoes, and extremely long red hair. As expats, we often referred to kandoorahs as 'rent a tent', which gives you an idea of their style.

Despite their lack of enthusiasm at my arrival, I was offered tea and coffee, so I chose tea. What I ended up with was almost certainly tea, although its taste was masked by what must have been half a ton of sugar coupled with condensed milk, to the point it tasted disgusting. It was all I could do not to throw up.

Before this appointment, I had attended others that same day, and as each progressed I began to realise that my presence was simply a 'trophy', someone for the men to stare at. I later found out that I was viewed as 'that type of Western Woman' (one considered to have low moral standards).

Back at the oil company, I met with two techies from their IT department. As is customary in England, I held out my hand, ready to shake theirs in formal greeting, though both men staunchly refused—something for which I had been unprepared—and there was an awkward moment whilst I pulled myself together and withdrew my hand, before continuing with the meeting.

When I returned to the car, I asked my chauffeur why those men had refused to shake my hand.

"Oh, Madam," he'd said in an apologetic tone, "these men (Muslims) think that women are unclean, just like pigs are unclean, so they won't shake your hand because it will make them unclean."

I couldn't believe what I was hearing.

"What?!" I exploded. "Who the hell do they think they are? I have mixed with big movers and shakers in the field of IT. I have sat with industry experts and run sales campaigns with dozens of men reporting to me, yet these two bearded men think I am a pig!"

The chauffeur provided no further comment.

Light-hearted Solution?

A few weeks later, I returned to the oil company in Kuwait, this time with my technical team. I knew I would meet the same men as before because they had specifically requested the presence of male technical staff this time. Even still, I had a presentation which I fully intended to deliver, though there was to be a twist. Before the meeting I had briefed my colleagues so they knew what the 'added extras' were and what to expect.

The presentation was going smoothly as planned. Then, partway through my carefully articulated solution and midway through a sentence, I stopped speaking and instead snorted like a pig. Deliberately. Subsequently, I continued with my presentation, only to stop and do the same thing again several sentences later. Confusion crossed the techie's features. The next time I decided to snort, I aimed it deliberately towards the two men who had refused to shake my hand. I watched their faces as comprehension dawned. They knew something was happening, yet they had no idea what; meanwhile, my colleagues were barely suppressing their tears of laughter.

After the event finished and management departed, I was left alone with my colleagues and the two clueless techies from the oil company. It was time to twist the knife.

"Please excuse me," I said calmly, "I will leave you with my technical staff. I know that will be easier for you, and the last thing I want to be is piggy in the middle." With a final snort, I left.

To this day, I don't know if those poor chaps realised what was going on, though even if they did, they must have seen the funny side because we were awarded a rather large contract.

- 10 -

A Different World

Some years later, as I began to appreciate the culture more, I understood that the perspective the chauffeur had given me at our first meeting was somewhat distorted. He had shared with me how women were regarded, yet he was a non-Muslim. A fact I hadn't fully appreciated. The more I learned, the more I realised that the chauffeur had not possessed the depth of understanding I would come to attain – despite having lived in the region for twenty-seven years.

The real reason the techie men didn't shake my hand was because it is not allowed by Islam for a man to touch a woman to whom he is not related, i.e., mother, wife, sister. When it became clear that the chauffeur had been mistaken, I felt (and still feel) embarrassed about my role in disseminating an untrue statement, as I relayed it to many others. I now recognise that it did nothing to bridge the divide between the culture of Arabs and the Western world.

As expats, we often lived with the fear of being deported should we upset a local. Those of my compatriots who purported to speak Arabic told tales of the Friday reading (Khutbah) when locals would chant hatred towards expats. Of course, with my ignorance and naivety, I bought into this in the same way I bought into women being considered dirty, yet I had no proof that this was true either. Sadly, because I believed what I had been told, my disdain for local Muslim men only deepened.

Compared to the UK, locals in Dubai lead a more laid-back lifestyle and are known for often being late. Whenever a new Muslim client approached my counselling business, I anticipated they would likely be late to every appointment. Having been let down by this on several occasions, I chose not to take them on initially and would tell them I was busy which may sound harsh, yet in order for my business to survive, it was necessary. Every time they were late, it was inconvenient, and when they would eventually arrive, their appointment would inevitably overrun, affecting subsequent appointments. Coming from an English background, I found this working style challenging to navigate, which highlights how our way of life in the Western world differs significantly from the society in which I was running my business. That's not to say I wasn't accommodating – I recognised I was living in their country – yet I felt it essential to establish some boundaries regarding my business and time. Otherwise, I couldn't provide the help and support I so desperately wished to offer.

I remember one Muslim lady who came to see me. She complained that her husband had lost interest in her, and I remember advising (amongst other things) that she wear makeup. From personal experience, I often feel better if I spend time looking after myself, which can translate positively to those around me. I hoped that if she could regain some of her youthful pride, she would radiate this to her husband. Then she told me something I was in no way prepared for. Her biggest fear, she revealed, was her husband taking another wife. I know my face betrayed my shock.

"And divorce you?" I asked.

"No," she'd replied, "in addition to me."

That was my first introduction to the non-monogamous element of the religion. Muslim men are permitted to take up to four wives.

Leaving my First Marriage

After returning to Dubai in 2007, my first husband and daughter eventually flew over to join me. I was delighted to see my beautiful Kitty again, though I had a heavy sense of dread regarding my husband. I knew I couldn't continue the relationship when my heart was so broken, yet I couldn't bear to hurt Kitty. In the end, I persisted with the marriage for a further year, and my husband was none the wiser. He thought everything was fine but it wasn't. Above all else, the trust had gone.

Prior to their return, I had been crunching some numbers to work out the viability of leaving the marriage. I discovered that if I saved enough from delivering training courses and working with private clients, I could begin divorce proceedings, safe in the knowledge that I would have financial freedom. In theory, it worked, though it would take about a year to accrue enough money to make it happen. Until that time, we picked up our usual routine: Kitty went to school, I went to my clinic (which included the endless battle of traffic in Dubai), and my husband went wherever he went. Outside of work I continued to tread water, waiting for the day I could support myself and Kitty.

Then, one day, eventually, it happened. My divorce was final, Kitty and I were financially independent, and I had everything I believed I wanted. The only thing missing was a life partner.

Until Ramadan 2008 – which is when everything changed.

Ramadan 2008

Ramadan is an annual pillar of the Islamic religion. It occurs during the ninth month of the Muslim calendar. The exact dates change year on year, though it always lasts for one month and is celebrated with a time of strict fasting from dawn until sunset each day. One rule that must be respected during Ramadan is to abstain from eating or drinking in public. As a Western woman, it was not always easy to remember to observe this, and I would sometimes sneak a drink of water in the car on my drive to work. The good thing was that the roads were generally quieter, so avoiding being seen was a little easier.

During this time, I found myself in the local police station—not because I'd been caught sipping water in public, far from it - I needed to renew my driving licence.

After the disaster of my first marriage, I had prayed for a good husband, and it was on this day, as I sat waiting at the police station, that I met my soon-to-be second husband. For us to meet in such an odd location felt like a sign; this, I believed, was the man I had been waiting for—the good husband I had manifested. For so many years.

Meeting my Second Husband

My first impression of him was, 'Wow, what a good-looking man!'

He was very cute, and the UAE national dress was a real turn-on. He smelled wonderful, and just like that, I was smitten.

After we had exchanged pleasantries and then gone our separate ways, I was thrilled to receive a text a while later asking what I thought of him. Apart from commenting that he was nice, I can't remember what I said, though his response telling me that I was like "forty-seven degrees in the summer" was flattering. (I interpreted this to mean 'hot' rather than a situation to be avoided).

Two weeks later, he asked me to marry him. It was a whirlwind, and I had no doubts or fears when we said our vows on June 7th, 2008. I was totally in love.

After our marriage, we formed a routine. We would spend time together in my tiny office - Chex Tiny, as I called it – which became our coffee shop and restaurant. I remember cooking a Thai curry and then transporting all the dishes, plates, knives and forks, tablecloths, candles, etc., to my office for us to eat on the floor. He bought ice cream. I had never been so happy.

He would shower me with gifts, or rather second-hand presents: diaries from companies wanting to do business with the department where he worked, books given to him, an occasional present from when he had travelled, something of little value, though to me, at the time, it was wonderful. I was so caught up in the emotion of marrying such a good-looking, kind, thoughtful, local man that I overlooked what was staring me in the face right from the start – he was tight with his money. That's not to take anything away from him. He was a man of his culture, and when it came to his duties and obligations, he was absolutely a man of honour.

Embracing the Culture

Marrying into the culture only increased my interest in theology and Islam. Over the years, I have read many scriptures, including the Bible, the Bhagavad Gita, and those related to Buddhism. I have also studied Spiritualism, yet despite my connection with the Spirit world, I haven't found any theologies that 'hit the spot'.

Growing up, my mother's view of religion was certainly skewed. She told me that God didn't exist because He had been a 'bastard', abandoning her with three kids, no money, and a council house to call home. In those days in England, there was a certain 'stigma' attached to living in a council house because it conveyed to the outside world that you were essentially poor. Even though my mother was adamant about her disbelief in God, I still felt a calling towards religion and, against her wishes, attended the local High Church. Whenever I went, Valerie would mock me, repeatedly saying it was simply a 'phase' that I would outgrow. It was ironic, considering how many of my friend's parents would have loved their children to show interest in church – yet not my mother. Her negativity permeated all aspects of our lives, and I now believe that part of it stemmed from uncertainty. If my mother could 'prove' something, she would believe it, which is a sentiment that lingered with me into adulthood.

I think this is why I was searching for something to grasp onto. I needed to have that depth of belief in a system, if you will, a way to allow everything else to make sense, and I genuinely believed I had found that in my second husband, his religion, and his culture.

Sadly, the dream was not to be.

- 11 -

Learning To Listen

<u>When your intuition is screaming ...</u>

Remember I told you that intuition is everything?

One morning, before I married my second husband, my intuition was not good. It kept repeating the phrase *'from the frying pan, into the fire,'* and I had no idea what that meant regarding me and my life. Despite my previous advice to 'listen to your intuition,' I chose not to listen to mine that day. I ignored it.

We had been married for about five years when I began to sense that something was wrong. I couldn't quite put my finger on it, though. In the back of my mind lingered the fear that he might wish to take another wife (I now realised that he was 'permitted' to take four wives, and I was the second), but I consoled myself with the knowledge that he had neither the time nor the money to do so. Until that fateful day.

It began like any other. My husband went to his car to leave for work. He started the engine, shifted into reverse, and then uttered a few words just as he was about to depart. Words I had been dreading and praying I would never hear.

"I'm hesitating to tell you, honey," he'd said.

"What?" I had asked.

"I am thinking of getting married," he'd replied.

It's worth taking a moment of pause here to remember my client, all those years previously, who had been frightened of her husband doing this very thing. At that time, I'd been shocked, and now, after spending so long immersed in the culture, I had come to know this for what it was—routine. My response, therefore, was perhaps not what you would expect.

"Have you married someone else?" I asked.

"No, not yet."

"For you to feel this, it must be written for you," I'd said. "Can we talk about it? Come back into the house so that we can talk."

"No," he'd responded, "I don't want any questions." And with that, he was gone.

I watched in a state of shock as he continued reversing out of the drive, leaving me once more as he set off for work. Back inside the house I started crying, my brain going into overdrive. What does this mean for Kitty and me? Where will we live? Will he divorce me?

I called him, and he answered in a resigned tone.

Me: "What does this mean for Kitty and me?"

My husband: "Well, it will be difficult for me to maintain three houses, and I won't be able to give you any time".

Three houses. For clarity, I was the second wife; the third (new) wife would require a house, and with his first wife housed separately, my husband would need to pay for the upkeep of all three. Religion permitted the men to take four wives on the proviso that he must treat them all equally. My husband was saying that to afford to maintain a third property (and treat us all equally), he would need to work more and spend less time with me. I would also not receive (any) gifts. Terrified at the prospect of not seeing him, I gave the only answer I could.

Me: "That's fine. I will gift you my time. Does your first wife know?"

As I write, I reflect on how strange this conversation seems. I struggle to understand now how I was so calm and the situation so 'normal'.

My husband: "No, why? Will you tell her?"

Me: "No, why would I want to be the cause of any fitnah (bad feeling)?"

My husband: "Okay."

Me: "Please don't divorce me, I love you."

My husband: "Okay."

On the next Friday, he came to me as usual, and we went to the Brr (desert). As we passed an area far from Dubai, he pointed to some buildings where Chinese immigrants typically live.

"Go and live there," he said. "I will give you 50,000dhs. I promise that I will pay for your rent and your car. I want you to divorce me."

If I had been shocked before, I was even more so now. "I don't want to," I said. Tears formed in my eyes, and I couldn't prevent them from falling.

"Why are you crying?" he asked.

"Sorry! Sorry!"

It was impossible for him to understand why I was crying. Moreover, he expected me to be elated at the news that he would be taking a third wife - yet I was not. His request was far from unusual in his culture, though there was also a belief that if a husband could not divide his time fairly, he should focus on only one wife. It was then I realised he was financially unable to take another wife. He wanted me out of the picture so there was one less person to sustain and one less person to spend time with. What galls me now is that I accepted the situation, even begging him to stay. Partly because I loved him deeply though mainly because I was fearful of not being able to support myself and Kitty. At length, he suggested a solution.

"Why don't we split your house in two," he offered. "You have half, and she can have the other half."

Readily, I'd agreed. It would be a logical solution that wouldn't cost him any more money, and I would be able to remain his wife.

Despite its perceived affluence, Dubai is as affected by economic downturns as the rest of the world, and my husband decided to take his third wife during such a downturn. My house had been purchased when the prices were booming, so I knew he would lose money if he were forced to sell it at that time. Equally, I didn't have any means to support myself and Kitty, so remaining in our home, even if only half a house, meant we could survive – and survival was everything.

Another day passed, and as usual he came to me at the normal time. He said he didn't want to change his routine for fear of arousing his first wife's suspicions. I think he was surprised at my reluctance to divorce. I believe he expected me to agree and move out so that wife number three could take up residence. What interested me was his determination to keep his third wife secret from his first wife, hence his suggestion to maintain the same routine. He did not want to arouse any suspicion.

When we got married and I became his second wife, I knew how difficult it was for his first. My husband told me how painful and humiliating it had been for her, leading me to wonder if he'd been secretly hoping to just swap number three for me, which would allow him to retain only two wives, and number one would be none the wiser. My refusal to obtain a divorce had put a spanner in the works.

I had tried to explain the pain to him; it fell on deaf ears. He offered no empathy or consideration for my feelings, simply casting me aside in anger whilst commenting that my reaction had been 'exactly the same as his first wife'. And that's when I knew he had already taken a third wife, despite what he'd told me.

She was younger, no doubt, and would, in all likelihood, produce more heirs. That much seemed obvious. He would dedicate more of his time to her, and it wouldn't only be his first wife feeling the pain of his absence. I would be feeling it, too.

I couldn't stop crying. In a few days, I lost 3 kgs and considered marketing my weight loss as "The Third Wife Diet".

I couldn't sleep or focus on clients. My life, which I had thought was okay, was now turned upside down. It was a complete mess. I felt both helpless and hopeless. I had married a man who, in my view, had been knowingly deceptive. Although I was his second wife, I genuinely believed I was the only woman he desired. When we began seeing each other, I am ashamed to admit I didn't consider it from her perspective. For me, it had been exciting, an illicit affair that we kept to ourselves. Although there was no physical relationship or even holding hands until after our marriage, I had convinced myself that this behaviour was 'normal' for men like my husband, yet even with that understanding, I naively held onto the belief that there would never be anyone else. It took him ten months to inform his first wife about me, and even though I was glad our secret could finally be revealed, I felt sadness and sympathy for her. I am sure she had thought she was the only one he needed, too. Part of me rejoiced in having him, though another part was considerate of how difficult that time must have been for her. Whenever I considered the challenges she might be facing, I reassured myself that she would have expected him to take another wife. It was part of the religion.

Now that I found myself in exactly the same position, I realised I had massively underestimated the impact. Being on the other side, to be the one who was now going to be an outcast, felt so very different. Shame for how I had minimised his first wife's pain engulfed my emotions, almost in tandem with the hurt I experienced, knowing that he was moving on.

When we'd first met, my husband would visit daily for three hours. As my feelings grew, I wanted more of him, so I began to ask if he had told his first wife. I still remember the relief when he confirmed he had done so, yet that niggling sorrow for her lingered.

"Why don't you smile?" he'd asked, confused at my sadness when he had done what I'd been requesting for a long time.

"Why would I smile at someone else's suffering?" I'd replied.

That sadness was short-lived, though, because it was only now, with him taking his third wife, I began to realise how little I had appreciated the depth of his first wife's pain.

- 12 -

Learning To Live with Pain

One of the worst parts of the whole third-wife situation was the fact I had lost my financial independence. This I had surrendered gladly upon our marriage, and now I had little to prop up myself and Kitty. Almost as much as it hurt to lose him, it hurt to realise I was trapped with nothing and no means to get out.

My lifelong friend, Jeanette, had always harboured reservations about my second husband, yet I had been too blinded by love to listen. It's often the way when you eventually see the light of day, though by then, it's too late.

When I told her that he was going to take a third wife, Jeanette had been consumed with anger, punching a hole in the wall in madness at what this man had done to me. I cried and cried on the phone to her, feeling helpless, trapped, lost and perhaps a little stupid. I had fallen for a cad, and now I was to pay the price.

His first wife, I think, dealt with the 'addition' of wives better than I. She made a point of befriending 'second wives' in the large extended family and had remained outwardly confident that though it was acceptable for her husband to marry another, he would always be hers. It transpired that this was an act. She hoped he would not take additional wives, yet when he did, she saved face by outwardly showing acceptance, which I later discovered was false. She was no happier about my arrival than I was about the arrival of number three.

Before I had come on the scene, my husband had already tried to take a second wife. His first wife had managed to thwart that attempt when she discovered the existence of the second woman. After confronting my husband about his intentions toward this second lady, she then proceeded to visit the office where the woman worked and caused a huge scene which put paid to any second marriage. When my husband told me this, he revealed he'd been courting this first 'second' wife for two years. Having the relationship brought out into the open made him realise he didn't want to fight for her and that he had essentially been miserable for the entirety of those two years. I took great reassurance from this story. It had taken him only two weeks to ask to marry me, so I must have been the only one for him; his feelings must have been incredibly strong. Right?

Wrong.

After our marriage, my husband spoke regularly of the need for his first wife not to be told. She had conceived a child during the 'first, second marriage' phase, and the baby's subsequent birth had been traumatic. Against my better judgement, I agreed to allow him one year to tell her, though, in the end, he told her of my existence after ten months.

Surprisingly, as the second wife, I was informed almost immediately about the plan for wife number three, yet he insisted once again that wife number one should know nothing about her. The pattern of keeping the first wife in the dark was repeated, and now I was part of the secret. This caused me nothing other than pain. I hated knowing that wife number three was waiting in an apartment somewhere for him to arrive, eagerly anticipating their time together and feeling the world stand still as he devoted his attention to her. In exactly the same way as I once had.

The addition of number three meant I barely saw him, with our time reduced to thirty minutes here and there. No longer did it feel special. No longer did I feel cared for. Now, all I felt was pain. It's like I was being offered the crumbs from his plate. My hasty agreement to give up my valuable time with him so that I could keep a roof over my head had played out in a way I could never have foreseen.

Focusing on Business

As a distraction, I invested in training myself to become a business coach. I've always enjoyed learning and welcomed the opportunity to improve my skills. For this, I joined a programme which became a life-saver. There were twelve people on this programme, which basically provided a framework for us, as business owners, to obtain work through referrals. We were all in the same boat – we needed business – and over time, I started to really feel like part of a community. The pain didn't necessarily stop, though; I was just able to mask it behind my traditional head coverings. I would often join the group with tears of pain, shock and betrayal pouring down my face, yet no one ever knew.

As well as referrals, the programme helped us with practical assistance in areas such as company image, branding, sales strategy and so on. This, for me, was crucial as I lived in fear of being thrown out of my home without any provision for income. My counselling clients had been wonderful, yet there was not enough of them to provide sufficient income for rent or to bring up my daughter; I needed to earn more money, and for that, I needed work.

One downside of this group was having to listen to their endless life commentaries – hearing all about their wonderful weekends and families. Even in a crowd of like-minded business people, I felt completely isolated and utterly alone.

Construction

The plans to chop my house in half continued at a pace, so Kitty and I cleared out rooms and disposed of belongings. This was so we could fit into the half-house we would be left with.

Increasingly, I found myself alone with my own company, reflecting on every word and action, gaining insight into who I was and what it meant to be human. These lessons held value, though as days turned into weeks and months, I realised they were lessons I could have easily lived without. In one half of the house that used to be mine in its entirety, my husband and his new wife were lying in bed, literally feet away. The pain was indescribable.

It did allow me to explore my Spiritual calling more, though. I began to appreciate that, as Spiritual beings, we leave behind our human existence when it is our time to do so—and by then, we will know what it is to be human. We will have experienced all of the ugly and beautiful emotions that go with human existence—whether we invited these emotions or not.

Lying in bed, I felt profound loneliness, knowing that my husband was in a different bed, holding tightly onto another woman. I'd always loved his hugs, the feel of his brown arms wrapped around me at night as he breathed gently into my ear. When I awoke to look at his rugged face, I was overcome by his beauty. To me, he had been the epitome of sexy—and now he was ensconced in the embrace of someone twenty-plus years younger than him.

One day, my husband called while I was at the cinema with Kitty and a friend. I had learned to adopt a cheery tone when speaking with him so that I could disguise my pain. We exchanged pleasantries, which struck me as odd, for he appeared to have no purpose for calling me that day. He spoke as if nothing had changed, and I found myself wondering how he could look himself in the mirror. He was still deceiving everyone in his life—his third wife, his first wife, and his family—and although he wasn't entirely honest with me either, I at least had more knowledge of the situation than all the others. As I reflect now, I realise how much of a fool he was, genuinely believing he could keep his duplicity under wraps.

I still don't know why he called that day. It was oddly unsettling and spurred me into action. I arranged to visit my husband's father that night to see if there was any hint he knew of his son's activities. Sadly, he was not at home with his first wife, so I visited his second wife on the pretence of asking about his health. She informed me that my father-in-law was with his first wife, out somewhere alone, which meant, if they were alone, that my husband was not with them. I already knew he wasn't with his first wife, for he was very rigid in his visitations to her, so I concluded he must have been with his third wife. Presumably, the earlier unexpected call had been to keep me sweet and ensure I maintained my silence.

That Friday, my husband visited for thirty minutes. When we sat on the sofa together, the pain he had caused me disappeared, and whilst I hated myself for it, I inhaled the drug of love like an addict, taking those precious minutes and living on a high, desperately waiting to get my next fix. The atmosphere between us felt good, so I decided to address the physical split in my home. To this day, I can remember the look of shock and bewilderment on his face.

"There are many things that you have said to me over the last five months which have hurt me," I said, "yet I think the worst must be when you told me that if I needed anything, I could knock on the door (to the other half of the house) as the maid would."

Though we laughed at how silly this sounded, I continued. "I would rather be bleeding to death on the kitchen floor than knock on that door like the maid".

My husband had no response, and I was reminded once more how most men appear entirely insensitive to women's emotions. He seemed to have no idea that threatening to put me in an apartment in the poorest part of town, throwing me aside like an old pair of shoes, and lying about his marriage and his endless deceit would hurt me. It was the most miserable time of my life.

On the odd occasion he came to the house and found me crying or upset, he found it impossible to deal with. He didn't understand why I was emotional and didn't ask what he could do to fix things. His only response was to leave – which did nothing except exacerbate the hurt.

Earlier in my story, I reflected on some of our stereotypical British behaviours. Another trait for which we are also well known is the 'stiff upper lip', a coping mechanism I was thankfully able to use during this challenging time. I put on an act to the outside world, pretending that everything was good and that life was happy and fulfilling. In reality, for the first two months of the 'third wife' period, I woke every day with a dreadful feeling in the pit of my stomach. It took me a while to identify the emotion, and when I did, I realised it was regret.

Regret that I was still alive. Because inside, I was dying.

Inevitably, I began withdrawing from life and stopped returning clients and my friends' calls and texts. They started to ask questions, so I would lie to cover up the fact that my heart was broken. I couldn't eat or sleep and would sit in meetings like a zombie.

Working Towards Independence

On Friday, January 17th, 2014, a date which preceded my husband legally marrying his third wife, I woke up at 6 a.m. It was the day of our garage sale—the one necessitated by my husband's desire to cut my home in half and move his third wife in. Alongside one of my dear friends and my daughter, Kitty, I watched as more than thirty people arrived to pick through my belongings. After a few hours of reasonable success, we ended the sale and travelled to the mall for breakfast.

Later that morning, Kitty and I decided to walk around a local park. As I was driving down the road from our home, my husband called, asking if we were near the house because that's where he was headed.

"Oh great," I replied excitedly, "then I will come back".

"No need, I am here to make some adjustments," he'd said.

Realising he must be visiting with his soon-to-be third wife; otherwise, why would he want me to stay away? I immediately turned the car around, my body shaking with adrenaline. Although it was not my house—as my husband continually reminded me—it was nevertheless mine and Kitty's home, and I wanted to see the woman for whom I'd been cast aside.

When she arrived, I maintained my calm exterior and greeted her with polite cordiality. There was no way I was going to feed my husband's ego further by causing a scene. She, too, spoke carefully as we sized each other up, me secretly pleased to find her a plain woman. I had imagined a buxom, big-lipped, over-made-up female, so I congratulated myself on how unremarkable she was. I remember thinking that I was much prettier than she. How shallow of me.

As he showed her around my home, it became apparent that she had little concept of the situation. Some of her comments were poorly chosen, if not immature, so I put on a show for her, holding my husband's hand and kissing him on the cheek. I wanted to send the message that I was still married to him and that she had been lied to, for I don't think she truly knew who I was. I smiled as I thought about the cuckoo – a bird that makes its nest in another bird's, even bringing up their young if the nest contains eggs.

Perhaps I was the cuckoo; perhaps she was the cuckoo. Whichever, one thing I was clear about was that I was unmoved. I was going nowhere.

Out of the Mouths of Babes

Throughout this ordeal, I maintained my composure, my mask only slipping later when I was alone with Kitty again. Without warning, she burst into tears.

"I don't want that woman in my house," she said.

It was the first time I understood how confusing this was for my beautiful, innocent daughter. She was effectively collateral damage, a girl growing into a young woman who was doing her best to cope and understand.

The following Saturday, my husband arrived for a flying visit, this time with yet another group of workmen. It seemed that the cutting up of my home would be a more significant project than he'd initially expected. Though each builder quoted the same price, my husband called in worker after worker, convinced he would eventually get the job completed more cheaply. Work had already begun on the 24th of December yet had ceased almost immediately as round after round of builders visited.

That night, as Kitty and I sat quietly, me massaging her feet, she said something so profound that I felt with absolute certainty it had come from Spirit.

"I just imagined you sitting there with white on, although I wasn't in white, only my sleeves were a cream colour," she said, "and I imagined that you were a pearl and around you were beams of light like a circle and people were throwing things at you that are black. The black hits you, and cracks appear in the pearl, then the Spirit sends light, and the cracks disappear, and it becomes whole and perfect again. Then, when it has another crack, it becomes a dent, and Spirit sends it even more light, and it becomes perfect again."

I froze. In awe at the purity of her words.

"I imagine two arms come out of this pearl," she continued, "and they pull me in, and then I'm inside a really plush hotel with all red carpets and ice cream. That's me protecting you. Do you know how pearls are formed?"

I can't remember my exact response, though I do remember having to swallow past a huge lump that had formed in my throat.

The Third Wife

By April 2014, my home had been split, and wife number three moved in. I had officially been usurped by a younger model. The situation was so bizarre I could barely comprehend.

To add insult to injury, my husband's attitude towards me had shifted. My once-loving partner became cruel, persisting in his fabrications as he moved from one wife to another. His first wife still didn't know there was a third, so he told her he was visiting me while he was with her – wife number three. His world became consumed by wife number three, and any calls or texts between us had long since ceased.

The loneliness was the worst. I imagined him having relations with her the way he did with me: holding her tenderly and telling her how much he loved her. As I faced this new version of my reality, my head became crowded with unhelpful thoughts.

In the early days of his third wife, I tried to keep the spice in our relationship. I would send him sexy texts, desperate to keep him hooked on some level, yet he never turned up when he said he would. The arranged meeting time would pass without a word, and then he would eventually show up, telling me to 'make it quick' as he only had five minutes. And it was literally five minutes – if that.

By now, I had begun to realise this man was manipulative. Once more, he would arrive, do his 'duty' as quickly as possible, and then go next door to 'her'. He would make excuses for needing to be with her so much, saying that her Wi-Fi needed fixing, for example. It didn't.

I would picture him downstairs with her, a big grin on his face, thinking how he'd just been upstairs with me. Then he'd return to his first wife and look her straight in the eyes, knowing she had no idea of the depths of his deception.

Looking back, I believe much of his behaviour was rooted in insecurity. He felt undervalued—perhaps at work—and needed to prove to himself that those who didn't believe in him or those who undervalued him were wrong.

He continued to come and go as he pleased, reading yet not responding to any texts I sent. I maintained my composure, with the angel on my shoulder observing and keeping count as I waded through unspeakable pain. Waiting – though I knew not for what.

On one memorable occasion, he was visiting, and as he went to leave, he invited Kitty to come with him and greet our 'neighbour' – wife number three downstairs. Then he poured salt on the wound, telling me I was welcome to 'come over any time' as if he and I were little more than neighbours.

Through the walls, I would hear him and his third wife laughing and watching TV. I would hear him shower after they'd been physical.

I see now with blinding clarity how he had swept me off my feet when we first met. I had been praying for a good man, and the timing was perfect. So perfect that I believed I had been sent one.

How wrong I had been. I literally did jump from the frying pan into the fire.

I wish I had listened to my intuition.

A Quick Deviation: Understanding Loneliness (Past and Present Day)

According to the Oxford English Dictionary, loneliness is a *'sadness perpetuated by having few friends or regular company'*. It leads to feelings of isolation and often hits unexpectedly, becoming particularly acute when no one else is present.

You can feel lonely even in a crowd. If you are with a group of business colleagues, friends, or family members with whom you struggle to connect, you will almost certainly experience a sense of isolation.

I've discovered that loneliness affects me most profoundly at the end of the day. This is the time when I realise I have no one to share the experiences of the day. Not only am I unable to impart my stories, there are also no stories for *me* to listen to and engage with. There's no one to discuss world events, politics, family, soap operas, celebrities, business, money, holidays, and so on with, and I am not the only one feeling this way. According to recent figures, a staggering 8.3 million people in the UK report feeling lonely, though I suspect the number is far greater. Many will not admit to their loneliness for fear of being perceived as weak.

During the COVID-19 pandemic, millions of people struggled with feelings of isolation. Though it is more socially acceptable to admit to these kinds of difficulties today, I still believe that we humans prefer to pretend that everything is okay—even if that means being on our own.

In my experience, overcoming (or coping) with loneliness comes from learning to live in the moment, enjoying simple things like the sound of birds singing, the smell of something cooking or the sun on our faces. Allowing these positive moments to permeate our minds will bring a measure of peace, and it is this peace which will enable us to move forward with more practical solutions, such as reaching out to groups or societies or trying a new activity. None of that is easy, though. I never expected to have such crippling times of loneliness, especially as I've got older, yet I try to look at the lessons I can learn from these moments. We all crave love, having someone to hold us and tell us it's all going to be okay, and if we don't have that 'person', navigating each day can be additionally challenging.

The main lesson I've learned is the importance of human contact and the value of friendships, particularly those around us who will always have our backs. Often, we can neglect these people when a shiny, new relationship or friendship comes along, so it can be helpful to remember how quickly we could lose that new connection, leaving us once more alone. Only this time, we might not have anyone to help us pick up the pieces.

The other thing I've learned is that those who are in extremely challenging and difficult relationships and situations often crave solitude. For them, it is the opposite problem. They face too many demands on their emotional health, which can lead to an impulse to escape and find some headspace and clarity.

Though these two scenarios are in many ways the polar opposite of each other, there is actually a lot of synergy. It can be useful in either situation to take a moment to think about those who are in our lives and why we keep them with us. Asking ourselves hard questions such as, *'Do I really like this person, or do they just fill a gap in my life?'* or *'Does this person add to my happiness?'* or *'How would I feel if I never saw this person again?'* and answering them honestly, can sometimes bring about the greatest reward. Somebody recently told me, "It's better to have someone than no one". I disagree. This person was suggesting they would rather have an affair than be on their own – an affair is a situation which brings untold hurt to so many people.

Yes, we might be alone, lonely, or struggling. As with the other themes in this book, I firmly believe that the answer lies within ourselves. If we can get to the root cause of our feelings of loneliness and isolation and work out their origins, we will be taking the first positive step towards a positive resolution.

Expiry Date

It had become apparent that my husband was going to use any means he could to get me out of the house and his life. Yet he wanted it to be my decision so that he could save face and pretend he had tried to do everything he could. He became nasty and unkind, yet I didn't budge. He had a responsibility to me, and I would not let him off that easily.

I found myself waiting for the day his first wife would discover the presence of wife number three because I knew she wouldn't pull any punches. I wanted to watch him fall and then realise, too late, that I would not be there to catch him again. I wanted him to understand the pain he had caused and the people he had hurt, so I became subtle with my messages to others. I hoped they would see my turmoil, realise my disconnect with life, and start to understand what was going on for me and for Kitty. I wanted so badly for the word to get out.

I heard friends talking of other men, kind men, and I wished I had such a man as an example for Kitty. I didn't want her to grow up believing that the spineless man I had married represented how love should be.

The change in my routine was stark. Where I would spend hours with my husband eating, talking, and sleeping, now I was forced to listen to this playing out next door with someone else. I became an observer of my former life. We'd had our routine; it had been my life. We would watch movies together, and I would massage his feet, believing that to be something he loved - I was wrong. I mentioned it to him during one of his flying visits, encouraging him to stay awhile and let me massage his feet like I used to. He'd cut me dead.

It had been my assumption, he'd said, that he enjoyed me massaging his feet. It was an assumption only and was not the truth.

The tone of his voice cut me to the core. It had been another falsehood, allowing me to believe this simple act had been a beautiful part of our lives together. The way he spoke with disgust was unconscionable. More pain. Each time, he would dig ever deeper into a raw open wound.

Once, after a period of extended silence, I received a text message asking if I was busy. He wanted to come over for dinner. I was immediately concerned. This was far from usual, and I couldn't imagine what he had to say.

When he arrived, everything seemed normal. He moved about the house while I waited on tenterhooks for him to deliver his message. Was he here to insist we move out? Or was it something else? Was he sick, perhaps?

My friend Jeanette had predicted that something awful would happen a long time ago, and I felt that this could be it—this could be the time her prophecy came true.

I also knew that his third wife was away, and his first wife was likely at the beach with their children. I guessed he was coming to me because there was no other option. Taking my cues from him, I ate and talked as if everything were normal.

The time we'd spent apart meant I was beginning to see him in a different light. On that day, I stole a few side glances at him, noticing that where once he had looked like God's gift to women, now he was looking older and less attractive. A new bald patch was becoming more visible.

I watched my husband walk to the bedroom as we cleared the dishes, knowing exactly what he wanted. I went and did my duty, making sure to do everything he liked. Then, as was his custom, he showered, bade me goodnight, and left. The interesting thing was that this time when I stared into the blackness alone, I felt different. I knew I was finally becoming stronger. Moreover, I was learning to play him at his game, and all that mattered was doing whatever was needed to keep a roof over mine and Kitty's heads. The fact that my husband was too wrapped up in himself even to realise it made me smile. Slowly, I was moving away from him.

I'm unsure exactly when it happened: the realisation that he was misguided. He genuinely believed he could maintain three wives separately and pretend to his first wife that the third didn't exist. As for his third wife, he acted as if he no longer visited me. As wife number two, I was stuck in the middle and the only one with all the facts.

I wondered if the three of us were more similar than I'd first thought. Were we all gullible? Led by our hearts rather than our heads? Did we fall for his looks, knowing that he was telling us only what he wanted us to hear?

When I expanded on this thought, I realised that our differing cultures do not matter. At our core, we are all the same. Some seek a knight in shining armour, others a protector, and many a provider, yet **one thing remains constant among every woman I have ever known: we all want to be loved.**

As I grew in strength and remained calm, it amazed me how clueless my husband actually was. He believed that I was happy with the few crumbs of time he offered, along with the changing of my status from wife to mistress. Though I hated to admit it, I had become an enabler by this point, allowing myself to slip into the 'other woman' role and watching the various deceptions continue to unfold. Yet I had little choice. I was still powerless to make any real changes, especially having Kitty to protect as well. I knew I would endure anything I needed to until the time was right for us to leave.

- 13 -

Deserving More

By 2009, Kitty's father (my first husband) had remarried and was living in a neighbouring country, which meant Kitty could still maintain a relationship with him. That all changed, though, in 2016, when he declared that he was moving to Thailand. He told Kitty the night before he left, after which time he stopped sending money—basically abandoning her.

As someone once said to me, *'You really know how to pick them!'*

I have realised now that, yes, I *had* picked them, though not through my conscious self. They had been picked (for me) at a higher level so that I could face particular challenges and learn my (pre-ordained) life lessons.

Since this realisation, I have developed a mantra which I use to remind myself what I need, want and deserve and to protect myself from going to such a dark place again.

'I deserve and want better for myself. I want to achieve - and not just things in the physical world, i.e., a roof over my head and food on the table. I want a man I can talk to and share a bright new world with. The future that I want. I trust this man is out there.'

During one of my trips in 2014 (for Kitty to see her father), I remember pondering how much it hurt to know that my second husband lived less than twenty feet away from me (with wife number three in the other half of my house) and yet couldn't even greet me as a common courtesy. He claimed to love me, yet how could he when he had caused such immeasurable pain?

By pure accident, I'd once seen his third wife alone, and she looked miserable. I didn't know her well enough to recognise if that was her usual expression, though I sensed not. I wondered if she was unhappy. If she was, how could that man continue to live with himself, knowing all the heartache and suffering he had caused?

One Thursday night, he caught me off guard. He never visited on a Thursday, which clearly meant something was happening with his first wife since he typically spent Thursday nights with her. Although he never elaborated on why he was there, I was certain he would have spun an appropriate tale for wives one and three.

It's strange to recount that in six years of marriage, with the exception of that one night, I never woke up to my husband on a Friday morning.

Reaching Out to Spirit

At this point, I was struggling so much with all the mind games, secrets, lies, and uncertainties that I began to plead with the Spirits for help. I asked them for a solution, a way out. I was desperate to escape. I now knew this man for who he truly was. Selfish. He only wanted me there when no one else was around and to serve as a fallback for the day when his first wife finally uncovered his third. I wasn't willing to be that woman. Not anymore.

It sounds simple: Leave. Go. Do not return.

Yet my guides told me, "Wait, be patient; the timing is not right."

Recognising the Truth

I believe he was also searching for something he would never find. He would tell me that he didn't feel loved as a child, that other women belittled him in the past, and that his first wife took advantage of him, leading me to think that all he sought was the love I was eager to give. I didn't desire money or status. I just wanted him. Sadly, he didn't only want me.

Looking back, I'm certain that he was struggling to maintain the pretence of having it all together. One day, he told me that he couldn't *'keep this up any more'* and that he *'had to be me',* which made no sense, and without context, I had no idea what he meant.

After those comments, his behaviour toward me started to change; he would go to mixed gyms (male and female - which was frowned upon) and started receiving massages from women. I'm sure this was when he began considering a third wife. I asked him as much in 2011.

It was September, just after my mother's funeral, and I asked him outright if he was looking for another wife. His reply I will never forget.

"50/50," he'd said, "you will be finished in a couple of years".

He was referring to my age and its impact on my ability to bear a child. The time when I would be biologically unable to provide him with a child was rapidly approaching, leading me to wonder if this was what he had wanted/expected all along. The subject had never arisen, nor had the event occurred. Did this make him feel less of a man? Would my marriage have been different if I'd conceived a child?

I didn't know then, and I don't know now.

What *does* make a man? I still wonder.

- 14 -

Struggling On

Life continued despite my struggles, and in 2014, I spoke to my husband again. I wanted him to know the cause of my suffering. Naively, I thought that perhaps it would make a difference.

"Why can't you be nice when you come?" I'd asked.

"You know me by now," he'd replied. "When you first saw the real picture, you said I was mean. Well, I am. That is in my genes, in my blood".

"So, it's just a matter of time until she finds out?" I asked, referring to his first wife. Though I am ashamed to admit it, we both laughed.

Emboldened, I decided to ask about his third wife. "What does she say about me?"

"Nothing," he replied.

"I mean about us," I clarified, "and why you don't come and see me."

"I told her that you gave up your time with me for her. She said you didn't have to do that. That I could come and see you whenever I wanted."

I took a deep breath, processing. This was a crunch moment.

"Why don't you then?" I asked.

There was a long silence, and I looked deep into his eyes.

"It will be a hassle for me," he stated calmly. "Coming and going, walking up and down the stairs. You know how I hate walking upstairs."

I was speechless. This was the first time I considered his lack of attention might be less about dividing his time between the three of us and more about not wanting to be with me.

Despite the pain, I ploughed on, taking this moment for the opportunity it was.

"I am suffering," I told him.

"What can I do to fix it?" he asked.

"Come for a day."

"A daaayyy...?" he replied, as though I was asking him to give me a pint of blood from his arm.

"I gave you my time," I continued, "because I was frightened you would kick us out of the house."

He'd shaken his head. "No," he'd replied, "I wouldn't do that."

"You told me you'd get me an apartment by the cement factory!"

He'd taken a long look at me then before walking out of the door.

"If you don't like it," he'd said in parting, "then go."

This conversation confirmed something that had been nagging me for a while—that my husband never truly loved me. He thought he loved me, yet I believe this love was embedded in me as a mother figure rather than a woman. He saw in me the opportunity to become a father again and to continue to witness the purity of a mother's love for her child.

When he realised I couldn't give him that, he searched for another.

I'd sit there listening to him visiting with her again. I'd hear his voice in my head inviting me over to meet her, suggesting we become 'sisters'. I'd felt sick to my stomach.

"Never," I'd replied, shaking my head. "Never."

In May 2015, my father-in-law unexpectedly visited. His wives had encouraged him to come, and when I opened the door, I greeted him with a familiar kiss on his forehead, a sign of respect.

As he walked in, he came face to face with the wooden divide.

"This is your house?" he queried, somewhat confused.

"Yes, Dad," I replied.

"What happened?" he pressed.

"Oh, you will have to ask your son."

"Is he downstairs?"

"No".

"Did he rent the house out?"

"No".

"Where is he?"

"You will have to call him."

My father-in-law made the call, and I sat with his wives, waiting. They looked uncomfortable and sad for me.

"He hasn't worked out what has happened," one of them commented.

"Tell him," I replied.

Nobody would.

In an honour/shame society, it simply wasn't done. Instead, everything was brushed under the carpet courtesy of a tribal system where men were still considered superior. To go against this, to share a secret or untruth would be to go against the tribe. It would land you in hot water – so no one said anything.

Shortly afterwards, my phone rang. It was my husband.

"Why didn't you tell me you had invited Dad round?" He asked.

"I didn't; he just turned up. He is asking a lot of questions."

"What did you say?"

"I won't lie for you," I replied. "Though I won't tell him unless asked directly."

"Tell Dad you have a friend who has moved in downstairs." He instructed. (What a weak man).

"No. I won't lie for you."

"Then tell him you have a new neighbour."

"No," I replied.

I heard him sigh at the other end of the line as if his fate was sealed. If I didn't lie for him, then the truth about his third wife would come out, and his first wife would no longer be in the dark. The fact that he was so scared of his first wife was, to me, unreal.

I thought back to a time when my husband and I were sitting next to each other on the sofa. His first wife had phoned him, and I could hear her rough, high-pitched voice. As she became more agitated, my husband visibly shrank deeper into the sofa, a classic gesture designed to protect us from fear. He was scared of her, scared of his first wife.

Shortly after she found out about me, she began going out without warning, sometimes leaving the children without food. On one occasion, she told my husband that they were 'his children' and that he could *'do the shopping and cook them some food'*–to punish him for taking me as his second wife.

It's laughable to me now how I responded back then.

"Well, you didn't do anything wrong, Honey, you can take another wife." I'd said.

Now, I have a very different view.

Time passed, and by August 2015, life was carrying on painfully. When I heard him arrive, I would sneak a glance out the window and watch him pull up in his high-end car. Despite everything, I still felt excited when he came to me instead of her. I only had to see him, and time stopped – cliché, I know. A nuclear bomb could have detonated, and it wouldn't have mattered. In those moments, there was only him, and I hated that I still felt that way.

- 15 -

Women and Power

Before continuing, it would be helpful to add a note about **Religion** and **Culture** and their differences. Although they can be used interchangeably, especially when discussing religions and cultures other than our own, it's important for me to illustrate how the two differ:

For example, Islam states that women should be covered from their heads to their feet. Following the *religion* would mean women covering themselves as stated.

Whereas...

In Middle Eastern *culture*, a woman might wear a black Abayah dress, whereas in Western *culture*, she might wear a loose top and loose trousers.

Similarly, in the *religions*, men are allowed to have up to four wives. However, some *cultures*, such as those in Tunisia and Pakistan, do not permit this, irrespective of *religious* beliefs.

Cultural Differences

And so, it transpired that, like the seasoned storyteller he was, my husband created a 'new neighbour'. He could not have been more distasteful to me at that moment.

A woman who once visited my clinic told me something that, in many ways, put my struggle into perspective.

"The man," she'd said, "might be the head of the house; the woman, though, is the neck."

She was right. Essentially, it's all about men maintaining honour and avoiding shame, a concept that is completely alien to Western women.

For example, if a man of this religion bought a gift for his second wife and not his first, his first wife would complain to her sister-in-law (the wife of her husband's brother). She would do this knowing that the brother would then reprimand her husband because his wife (the brother's wife) had caused him (the husband's brother) distress. The brother would be less concerned with the unfairness of the gift-giving than with being subjected to his wife's sharp tongue for actions that were not his own.

In this society, a man's worth is measured by how well he looks after his family, *which includes how well he controls his wife's tongue.*

If the first wife spoke negatively about her husband, it would suggest that he was not managing her well, which would make him appear weak. Therefore, he would give her what she wanted to keep her satisfied. This is where the neck-and-head scenario originates. The neck connects the head to the rest of the body and must remain in place for the head to function.

For a first wife, it is bad enough when their husband takes a second, and even though their religion permits them to marry four women, with each additional wife, the first is made to look worse. This is why the first wife is often happy when the second and subsequent wives suffer.

When I met my husband, he told me about his first wife. He explained that she had left school at 16 without completing her education and had fallen pregnant with their first child a month later. He told me she had been 'so nice and lovely', yet the minute they married, she showed her true colours. Falling pregnant so quickly, he said, had sealed his fate. He often referred to their marriage as a prison sentence.

At the time, I felt sorry for this remarkable man, who had been trapped by a woman and was now stuck in a marriage of duty and obligation. I believed that I was his light and his sanctuary. What a load of nonsense.

When I began to see him for who he was, I realised that everything he had ever told me about his first wife was only seen through his perspective and, thus, not necessarily true.

In 2008, during the height of my love, my husband asked how he could get a British passport. He wanted me to 'call' someone and make it happen.

I explained that it didn't work like that; you had to be domiciled in the UK for three years and have proof of address. His response that day went unnoticed, blinded and deafened as I was by rose-tinted spectacles and earmuffs.

"You're no good to me then," he'd said.

Why had I not listened?

Finally Understanding What I Really Wanted

The one thing that always appealed to me about living within a different culture was the opportunity to become part of a big family. My childhood had been far from settled, and though I had my grandmother as my rock, I had never really felt like part of a family unit – which was something I desperately wanted.

My first husband's family had not accepted me – though I still, to this day, don't know why. Maybe I was too outspoken. There was one occasion when I shopped for and cooked a full three-course Sunday lunch for my first husband and his family. After they had eaten their fill, everyone congratulated my husband on how great the meal was even though he had done nothing towards it. He didn't bother to correct them, and I said nothing out of fear of sounding churlish.

I have also realised that with my father absent in hospital and then subsequently dying, I was looking for a father figure – someone who could protect me the way I believed my father would have done. Through my work, I have now come to understand that I was suffering from something known as the 'Cinderella Complex'. Many women, even in these days of female empowerment, fall victim to this, which can be described (according to Amazon) as:

'The psychological desire of many women to be taken care of, to have someone else take the responsibility for them, and the need for women to re-educate themselves out of such dependency.'

I know that when I met and married my first husband, that's exactly what I was looking for: someone to take care of me. Yet I forgot that I also needed to feed my soul.

When his infidelity finally ended our marriage, I wanted a man who could nurture my soul, one who was Spiritually enlightened, which is how I fell head over heels in love with my second husband. I believed I had found everything.

As you can see, I hadn't.

Many years later, as I retell my story, I want to emphasise that this book is not about me; it's about you and how what I have learned can help you face difficult challenges and the inevitable less-than-perfect moments in life. With that in mind, it's time to turn this around and address the next part of my journey. I need to answer those unasked questions and begin providing you with the **tools I used** to get from **where I was then** to **where I am now**.

- How did I get out?
- How did I reach this point in my life?
- And, perhaps crucially, how can what I have been through support you?

In the last few pages, I encourage you to reflect, find common ground, and listen to your intuition.

The answers, then, I am confident, will reveal themselves.

- 16 -

On Reflection

It would be beneficial at this point to summarise so that as you navigate your own journey, you can recognise the challenges I have faced and use my experiences as a guide. I'm not suggesting you follow my path; rather, I hope you take what you need from my story. You may directly relate to certain aspects, or you might simply grasp the feeling of helplessness that characterised my latter time in Dubai. Whatever you derive from my words, I hope you find encouragement, reassured in the knowledge that with the right support, we **can** make difficult choices. If I, who was more vulnerable and naïve than I realised, can emerge from such a journey, then so can you.

It was around September 2017 when I realised there was growing unrest within me. My life felt unfulfilled. With limited money in the bank and a husband who visited for a grand total of one hour a month, there was little to bring me satisfaction on a regular basis. It's not that I didn't work hard at our marriage—believe me, I did. I would text my husband every morning and every night, wishing him 'Good morning' and 'Goodnight', yet I received nothing in return (except for some air conditioning units, which he stated would not be given to wife number three). With everything I said or did, I had Kitty to consider, and I knew that she was, and would always be, my number one priority.

Kitty was by now sixteen and doing well at school. She received many letters of commendation – in total, twenty-seven by the end of her school year – indicating that she was bright and needed more than Dubai could offer at that time. She needed to access an education that would nurture her potential, and with universities being fairly new in Dubai (along with the restrictions that life placed on her there), it became apparent that for Kitty, if for no other reason, we needed to return home. To England. The problem was, how?

Making Plans

I began by increasing the frequency of our trips back home and finding legitimate reasons for us to return. Grandma's birthday, Grandma's illness, sister-in-law's party, family events- anything I could use to enable us to travel without difficulty. Having family reasons that satisfied my husband was not the only issue. I held an Emirati passport, which required an electronic visa waiver form to be completed 100% accurately. Unfortunately, I had mistakenly written a '1' instead of an 'I,' which resulted in Kitty and me being turned away at check-in and having to return to our home in Dubai. We then had to wait two days (the obligatory requirement) before returning to the airport and boarding the plane again. Those two days felt like some of the longest of my life as we sat waiting, staring at the television, desperate to get back to England.

We had already packed up most of the house. During our increasing number of trips, I gradually removed bits and pieces and took them back home to England, intending that we would have all of our stuff back in the UK before my husband even noticed we had not returned. The mix-up with my visa added to what was already a tense situation, so in the future, I made sure to have either Kitty or my friend Kerry check that I had completed everything precisely as it should have been.

Each time the plane landed on British soil, I felt relief wash over me. The green of nature was welcoming and bathed me in its healing, particularly when we reached the Lake District, where we always headed.

Though renting properties on each visit was expensive, it was definitely worth it to feel that sense of serenity and calm, knowing that one day, we would both be able to rebuild our lives and turn the pages of our next chapter.

While we were in the UK and before making a permanent move, I had a gentleman come in to look after my cats in Dubai. On one occasion, he contacted me to say that the air conditioning in the house had broken, and it was sweltering. (Hence the aforementioned reference to air conditioning units!). I asked him to buy a fan to keep the cats cool. When I returned, my husband refused to arrange for the air conditioning to be fixed, saying it was too expensive. We were to make do with the fans. If I had any doubt that I was making the right decision, it was firmly quashed then. He was never going to be anything other than tight with his money. He was, however, honourable with what was required of him from his Islamic faith.

One of the most wonderful things about returning to England and the Lake District was the sense of normality. You forget how much freedom we enjoy here, and I relished those times when I felt unobserved, unheard, and un-followed. I could say what was on my mind without fear of retribution.

I also used this time to reconnect with friends and establish relationships because it was important to me to have a support network when we returned permanently.

During our visits, Kitty and I would walk around the area and look at houses we thought we might like to live in. One time, while walking around one of the many lakes in the Lake District, we spotted a house that I dismissed because it looked ugly. As fate would have it, I ended up living in this 'ugly' house and soon ignored such shallow observations. My home's location and incredible views far outweighed any perceived 'ugliness'.

The worst part of leaving England (going back to Dubai was necessary in order for my plan of 'leaving by stealth' to work) was the overwhelming sense of dread I felt on the plane ride back. It sharply contrasted with the excitement I had experienced during those early flights and days, leading me to draw on every ounce of resilience I possessed to maintain the 'everything is normal' pretence.

Jeanette supported me as best she could, though leaving her always manifested an overwhelming sense of loss. The moment the plane wheels touched the tarmac in Dubai, I felt nothing except dread and depression. I knew I needed to make my plan work – soon.

Carrying on life as 'normal' was incredibly difficult when the only thing I ever looked forward to was seeing my cats. I would continue with my work commitments, sponsor companies, spend time with my business partner, and enjoy the weather when it turned a little cooler, yet always in the back of my mind was the 'how'.

How much longer?

How was I really going to make it work?

How would we survive?

Spirit, Intuition and University

I have spoken about my connection with Spirit, and this, in part, helped to resolve the 'how'. I felt an overwhelming intuition that Kitty would make it into Cambridge University. I recall speaking with her head of sixth form (in Dubai) and asking if he thought she could succeed; he told me no. Imagine my delight several years later when I could inform him that not only had she attended Cambridge, but she had also achieved a double-first with distinction in behavioural sciences and psychology. He merely congratulated her, but that was sufficient for me. I simply wanted him to know that despite his lack of encouragement, Kitty had not only survived; she had flourished.

My plan started with a vision board in my bedroom, which I photographed and stored on my phone. It served as a constant reminder of our upcoming departure and the achievements that awaited us when we returned to England for good. This would occur once Kitty had completed her education in Dubai. While we waited, I would envision the beauty and serenity that was ready to welcome us back home.

I recall the summer of 2018 being particularly hot in England. One night, I sat outside my rented cottage, taking in the spectacular views, when a sense of calm settled over me. A weight lifted, and I found myself suddenly able to let go of all the past pain and suffering, witnessing my plan coming to fruition. I could see the proverbial 'light at the end of the tunnel', and it was this that sustained my Spirit as the logistics of my plan slowly, agonisingly, fell into place.

Our time to return home to England was finally approaching. Kitty and I were geared up for our big move, and we were beyond excited to start our next chapter. Passwords and bank accounts were updated, everything was discreetly packed … and then COVID-19 hit, and no one went anywhere.

Like the rest of the world, Kitty and I were stuck until it was safe to travel. Yet the immense suffering of many during this time put our inconveniences sharply into perspective. The fact that we couldn't travel to England seemed inconsequential when the number of people dying worldwide continued to rise.

Once it was safe to move about again and Kitty had completed her education, the next step was to travel to England, where I would help her settle into halls at Cambridge University.

Moving Kitty into her university halls at Cambridge was the easy part. I still had to return to Dubai to finalise my eventual departure, and I didn't know how my husband would react to the amount of time I had spent in England and my increased 'need' to travel. In many ways, this was a test run, and I prayed he wouldn't make an issue of my absence.

The day I returned to my apartment in Dubai after settling Kitty in Cambridge, I remember bursting into tears. I felt bereft and empty. Now that my daughter was thousands of miles away, what else did I have?

In summary, this:

- A flat that was effectively an apartment in a building site.
- A husband I rarely saw apart from the obligatory twenty-minute nuptials now and again.
- No money to call my own.

This period of time was definitely one of the most challenging.

In addition, the laws relating to the company sponsorship scheme in Dubai (in which I was involved) had changed. This meant the income I earned from sponsoring other companies was due to end. On top of everything else, it felt like salt being relentlessly poured into an open wound.

At length, I spoke to my husband about my desire to be nearer to Kitty. This was the truth. I also knew it was the rationale to which my husband was most likely to agree. The conversation went surprisingly well. In fact, he went so far as to rent a house for me in Cambridge, suggesting I move there for the entirety of Kitty's education.

His readiness to agree caught me off guard; I think he was likely so busy with wife number three at the time that he felt a blessed relief at having 'one less to deal with' for a while. I was under no illusion that I would be expected to return to Dubai once Kitty had graduated.

Time to Leave

As I made plans, my husband asked me how long I would be away.

Two years, I told him, without really thinking it through.

While I had been taking our personal items home over the last few years, moving furniture out of the apartment had been more difficult. The law in Dubai states that if you wish to move things out of your apartment, you have to get the landlord's permission. Many people used to run away without paying their rent, leaving the landlord in debt, so the idea was that if you were forced to leave your furniture behind, at least it could be sold to reduce the landlord's debt.

I began moving things to a friend's house and then to a storage unit in the Lake District. Now that my husband knew I would be moving back to England for an extended period, everything became a lot easier to negotiate.

The only problem was that he had no idea I did not intend to return.

- 17 -

Coming Home ~ July 2021

Finally, in July 2021, I was ready to leave. The return flight needed to go via Frankfurt, which meant that due to COVID restrictions, I would also need to stay in Iceland for 11 days.

I had booked my flight through a travel agent who told me there were no seats in Economy Class. This meant I'd had to pay 300% more to get a seat in business class. I didn't care. I was going home, and nothing would dampen the relief and excitement I felt. (As an aside, there were only 19 people on that flight, so the story about the lack of seats in Economy was just that—a story.)

Although I was returning to England, I was still wearing my abaya and headscarf, indicating I was a Muslim woman of faith. The stewardess asked me what I would like to drink, and when I said orange juice, she carried it towards me on a tray that was also laden with champagne glasses. Unfortunately, as she leaned to pass me my juice, the tray caught the edge of my seat, tipping six glasses of champagne all over me. The only one that hadn't spilt was my orange juice.

The stewardess was absolutely mortified; the worst possible thing you can do culturally is to cover a woman of faith in alcohol. Promptly, she burst into tears. I consoled her, insisting it was not a problem. In fact, I saw it as a blessing making it much easier for me to leave the country, my robes and my adopted cultural identity behind.

Given that I had to spend time in Iceland, I decided to make the most of it and fell into a regular pattern of visiting a vegan restaurant, sightseeing, going to Viking burial sites and admiring the handsome men, who all looked exactly how I would imagine Vikings had done.

Two days before I was due to leave Iceland, the chef at my chosen restaurant began explaining to me—in broken English—that a volcano had erupted. I was frozen to the spot, remembering the 2010 eruption, which billowed smoke all over Europe and grounded flights for two months. Luckily, this eruption was minor in comparison, and I was able to board the plane to London as planned.

I think one of the most pivotal moments for me in all of this was when I disembarked that day at London Heathrow, walked through the automatic passport system, collected my luggage, stepped outside and picked up a hire car. After putting all my belongings inside, I sat in the driving seat and cried. It was then that it hit me. I had escaped. Kitty and I had escaped, and I would never, ever return to the country I had once considered my home.

Cambridge

I spent three years in Cambridge and looking back; it was the best thing I could have done. Although I had never truly left England in my heart, re-adapting to the culture was going to take some time, so living in a multicultural place like Cambridge provided the perfect bridge between Dubai and my eventual home in the Lake District.

And I love Cambridge – the architecture, the people, the environment, the businesses, and the variety of shops and shopping available. One of the wonderful aspects of Cambridge is its flatness. I would go out for a walk each day and easily cover four miles. I grew accustomed to seeing dogs again (something you don't really encounter in Dubai), I became used to chatting with people (which isn't done in Dubai), and I appreciated the fresh air and freedom. It allowed me to build my business, and I could finally be open and embrace the part of myself that is a psychic/medium. I could once again tell the world how I connect with Spirit and that I could commune and communicate with them. In Dubai, this is, once more, forbidden. It was mind-blowing to be able to be honest about who I truly am, and I wondered if it was similar for others who had been marginalised when they were finally able to speak their truth.

I maintained my connections and business in Dubai while establishing myself in England. I began networking, meeting new people, and just enjoying life again. The freedom to control my own destiny was incredible after being denied it for so long.

The 'ugly' house I bought in the Lake District provided an additional source of income during my time in Cambridge. I treated it as an investment and rented it out, knowing that once Kitty graduated, one or both of us would return to live there. Now, that house is my home, and it is truly beautiful. The views are spectacular, and wildlife runs free.

That house feels safe to me. It feels like home, and as much as I enjoyed Cambridge, I am finally settled where I need to be.

A Happy Ending

I haven't mentioned my cats, which I left behind in Dubai. Though it broke my heart, I knew I would be unlikely to find a rental property in Cambridge that would allow me to bring them with me, so, at great expense, I flew them back to the UK and arranged for them to be adopted by a couple here. The last thing I wanted was for my beautiful cats to be abandoned in the sand. I hated saying goodbye but I knew they would be fine and go on to enjoy the best life possible.

When I first got back to England, my husband would text often. In a strange way, I did miss him, though it didn't take long for me to realise that he, his country and his culture were all a part of my past, which needed to stay exactly where it was. It was time to focus on my future.

Communication has diminished, and I no longer miss any aspect of my marriage. Instead, I focus on what I have here: my incredible daughter, the beauty of nature, and the freedom to finally and unequivocally be me. Being married to him provided me with so many life lessons for which I will be forever grateful.

- 18 -

Live For Today

Now that we have reached the end of my story, I would like to share something I have observed throughout my life and during my work:

Often, every single one of us finds ourselves living in the future.

This is not a failure. It is something we are hard-wired to do. While it can be beneficial in some situations, most of the time it can lead to our downfall because we are promising ourselves this 'nirvana', this perfect life that the anticipation of future events will bring about.

We make (internal) statements like:

- When I've got a boyfriend/girlfriend, I'll be happy.
- When I get that promotion, I'll be able to buy everything I want.
- When I buy my first house, I'll have so much freedom, and life will be amazing.
- When I have children, my life will be complete. I will have the family I've always craved.
- I buy a lottery ticket every week because one day I will win, and I know that money is the key to my happiness.

This is a select few; I'm sure you can see yourself in some of these statements and probably have familiar ones of your own.

There's nothing wrong with dreaming—we all dream of winning the lottery and having everything we ever wanted. The problem is that when we get there, our lives feel no different—no better and sometimes worse. You only need to research some of the stories from previous big lottery winners to realise that money is not the answer to everything. Far from it.

We Are Where We Need to Be

I want you to understand that you (and I) are exactly where we need to be right now. Even in the worst times, we are where we need to be, so wishing our lives away to an uncertain, unlikely and potentially unhappy future is pointless. It won't get us there any faster. If we take the time to slow down, we will realise that with our world unfolding in its own time, we are more likely to reach the **right** destination, not the one we **think we want**.

In my current work, many people tell me that they don't like where they are now. When I reassure them that they are exactly where they *need to be right now*, this often brings up emotions of anger and frustration. They don't understand how their life can be any different and why they are being forced to 'remain' in a place that makes them unhappy.

They want a cure – as we all do. When we feel trapped, fed up, sad, lonely, depressed, upset or unfulfilled, we want a solution, a way to make it better, not a collection of words that potentially minimise their suffering.

I completely understand. I totally get why this is not what they want to hear – and probably not what you want to hear, either. Yet, I also understand why we find it so uncomfortable to believe we are where we need to be.

If I can help you understand this, then you will be able to edge ever closer to that nirvana.

Miracle Cures?

Think about it. If we go to the doctor with a problem that has been niggling for some time, we expect a cure. A miracle cream or medication that will sort us out in five seconds flat. It feels uncomfortable when we don't get this or are referred to another provider or specialist. Not only are we still in the same place as we were when we visited the doctor, we are now in an additional state of uncertainty, and humans are not wired to cope well with uncertainty.

Yet – and you're going to have to trust me here - uncertainty is good. Discomfort is good. Because this means you are in a time of growth, a period where you are learning how to move forward, becoming more in tune with yourself and ultimately letting go of the things that have held you back. When you start to embrace this uncertainty and discomfort, you will often discover key information that can help you move forward.

It might, for example, not only be a fear of heights that prevents you from jumping out of a plane (attached to a parachute, of course!). It could also be that you have a reluctance to open yourself up to new experiences.

In line with my beliefs and presence in the Spirit world, I also know that everything happens for a reason – even if that reason is not obvious and may never become so. Your actions, deeds, words ... they have all contributed to where you are now, and those actions, deeds and words all happened for a reason.

This is not a belief shared by everyone, though personally, I have found whenever a difficult situation has arisen, it has provided me with the chance to learn something. It has taught me another lesson in becoming a balanced human. If those situations had not occurred when they did, I would not have received that lesson – hence why I always believe that everything, good or bad, happens for a reason. The difficulty can arise when we cannot decipher what that reason may be – simply because, as I've stated earlier, human beings don't cope well with uncertainty.

Are We All Alone?

As of the date of writing, our world has a population of nearly 8 billion people. Yet still, we often feel alone. What I want you to start realising, however, is that Spiritually, we are never alone. While physically we may not be near our loved ones, someone is always there with us Spiritually. They may not exist on the same earthly plane as us, so they are not visible in the way we see our family and friends, but we can still communicate with them, whether out loud or in our thoughts, and we can seek their guidance.

If you give yourself time – we're back to those values again – ***patience*** and ***tolerance*** – to listen, you'll be surprised at the advice you receive.

As we learn to hear and receive this advice, so more lessons will be presented to us. For example, my lesson at the time of writing this book (2024) is one of non-judgement. I'll elaborate.

Non-Judgement

We are wired by default to be wary of things that may pose a danger to us. Our amygdala (the brain's fear centre) is working constantly to decide if we are safe. Having spent the last 15 years in an environment where others are eternally competitive with little to no concern for those to whom they may cause harm, I have enjoyed returning to the UK and realising that the same mindset is not present here. I am learning, therefore, to withhold my judgment of others now that I am back in my homeland, where the belief system could not be further from the one I have left behind. I need to re-acquaint myself with British values, which will involve practising non-judgement of others.

You might wonder what I mean by lessons—how do you receive them, and how do you identify them?

We Are Always Learning

The good news is that everyone can receive these lessons or advice—it isn't necessary to be a Spiritual believer—because this advice comes from our *intuition*, the voice we all have inside our heads. This voice is our constant guide, the voice we should listen to above all else, and the voice that ensures we are never alone.

Everything that happens to us is presented for us to learn from—and the trick is to learn it the first time we hear it if we can. We need to allow each event in and experience the myriad of emotions—even the unpleasant ones—because that is where we will be challenged most. Ultimately, it is from this place that we will learn and grow.

Think for a moment about emotions such as betrayal, abandonment, jealousy, and deception, and consider a time when you experienced those emotions. What led to those feelings?

Compare it to placing your hand on a hot kettle.

- » You do it.
- » You touch the kettle.
- » You realise it's hot.
- » You realise it hurts.

- » Quickly, you remove your hand.
- » You resolve never to touch the hot kettle again.

It's the same with our difficult emotions. Often, these emotions hurt us deeply, so if we take a step back from our metaphorical kettle and consider why we are experiencing them, we can perhaps identify what caused them and if they are appropriate and/or beneficial to us.

It's like reverse engineering. We know how we feel and that we are in pain, so to prevent us from continuing to experience pain, we need to work backwards and figure out what happened at each stage. Eventually, we will arrive at the root cause or the lesson.

The kettle example may be overly simplistic; however, it effectively illustrates my point. By working backwards, we:

- » Move away from the kettle.
- » Run our hand under the cold water tap to help with the burn recovery and pain.
- » Consider what led to our hand being burned – we boiled the kettle.
- » We wanted to clean the kettle, which is why we touched it.
- » ***Make sure the kettle is cold before we touch it.***
- » We'd also just boiled the kettle for a cup of tea, though.
- » ***If the kettle needs cleaning, use the desire for a cup of tea as a trigger and remind yourself never to do both activities at the same time.***

The lesson in this example could come at either of the two points in **bold**.

Now, we can work out what we can learn and what we can avoid doing again. Then, once we've learned the lesson, we can acknowledge it and move on. That's not to say we won't experience the same challenge again; it's just that this time, we have a foundation to base our future responses on.

We know we survived it the first time (or second or third…!).
We can acknowledge that we survived it and remind ourselves that we've already experienced this.
We are *not* willing to experience the same outcome. Therefore, we *make a change at this stage* before it's too late.
Then, commit the learning to our memory banks and move on. We may experience it again, so we simply repeat the process until we have formed a new, positive habit around it.

Listening to our Own Voice

Faith and belief don't have to be religion. They can be whatever suits you comfortably—perhaps simply having faith in the universe. No one else gets to choose what we believe in and what paths our lives follow. I have experienced many different cultures and worshipped under many different belief systems, yet throughout every single one, it was my inner voice and Spirit that guided me—not that belief system.

The strongest voice of all—the one that kept me going, the one that made me get out of bed each day, the one that helped me to believe in myself and my business when everything seemed hopeless was my *intuition* - my own values and beliefs.

I know that no matter what happens, as long as we are true to ourselves, listen to what we say, and practice the values of *patience* and *tolerance*, we will all achieve our goals.

- 19 -

Learning Patience

<u>You can't choose your family</u>

Patience has been a difficult lesson for me. Although I feel I have nearly grasped the art of patience in all situations, I still "don't suffer fools gladly." Learning to respond rather than react has also been challenging, and I am willing to admit that I still have some way to go with this.

Often, I would complain to John about my mother. I would tell him how intolerant she was and how she was one of the most negative people I knew. John would always respond:

"Aren't you being intolerant of your mother's intolerance?"

It takes a moment to understand that statement, so sit with it for a second and then apply it to your situation. Hopefully, you will see the beauty of its wisdom.

Despite her negativity, my mother has been a significant part of my journey in life as it is through my learnings from Arab culture that I came to respect and accept her for who she was. I am much more measured when it comes to 'responding' rather than 'reacting', and although she remained one of the most pessimistic people I've ever known, her legacy affects me much less than it used to.

Valerie

I recalled living full-time with my grandmother, especially after my father had entered the care home, or rather, the 'home for incurables'. I remember visiting him and feeling scared about how he would appear. The place smelled dreadful, and my father lay in the last bed on the left row by a window, which did nothing to alleviate the foul air. As we entered, he recognised Mother and my eldest brother, then completely overlooked his middle child, his second son, before also overlooking me. He seemed to have no recognition of the two of us, although he did seem aware of who my grandmother was.

For reasons best known to her, Mother chose that moment to ask my dad for a 'fucking divorce', which made little sense to me at the time; it felt inappropriate and her anger unnecessary. I have since learned that women in the 1970s were unable to initiate a divorce. This, in part, explains her attitude and actions, I guess. Interestingly, women couldn't take out loans either. Thankfully, times have changed.

My mother, Valerie (as she insisted we call her because she hated the term mother, mum or anything like it), also harboured anger at being 'forced' to work to support three kids. Boy, did we pay for that! Life was pretty miserable, and the answer to everything was always "NO". No, I couldn't go on a school trip - we had no money. No, we can't have a Christmas tree - one year, nobody paid any interest to it, and that was it for the rest of our childhood. No, I couldn't have friends over to play. No, we can't have fireworks - they are a waste of money. See what I mean about negativity?

On top of that, Valerie would always insist that 'all men were bastards' and 'God didn't exist', so it's no wonder I was geeky and introverted by the time I was fourteen. I was consumed by fear, with barely any worldly knowledge, and desperately looking for love. Or at least, that's what I thought I was looking for, which is why I have included this anecdote. I want to paint a picture of who I was and perhaps enable you to identify with my search for... whatever. If nothing else, you can see how my mindset and lack of a loving home (except for with my grandmother) impacted some of the decisions I would go on to make in my adult life.

I've also realised the importance of motherly love, and I sometimes mourn the lack of this in my relationship with Valerie. It took thirty-three years for her to tell me that she loved me, and even that was done through a birthday card. Before that, any such card had been signed 'From Valerie'. According to my brothers, I got off lightly, living, as I mostly did, with my grandmother.

When the love of a mother is lacking or perceived to be lacking, this can be incredibly damaging. In my case, I felt, as I grew and matured, a desperate need for her approval, and though she is no longer around, I am saddened at how entrenched her negativity remained. Often, she would tell my then-adult daughter: "No, that's dangerous", or "No, you can't do that."

I don't even think Valerie knew she was doing this.

How Not to be a Mother

One thing I learned from Valerie was how (not) to be a loving mother, and I react strongly if anyone suggests I am like her. This is one of the areas I've worked on in the past with John's loving guidance, and I have also sought support from the Spirit world. Where once I wanted love and support from my mother, I now find it in The Creator, through his angels, guides – or by whatever means it reaches me.

This is why, returning to the point about the tree exercise, I can say with utmost confidence that I am nearly always correct in my interpretation of the tree my clients draw. I 'tune in' to their work, though it is not I who provides the guidance. This comes from The Creator.

My counselling chair, where the clients sit, is affectionately known as the 'crying chair' because I have found that it is only a matter of time before even the toughest clients let go and express their emotions. I am confident I can connect with them on such a profound level because I am guided not only by logic and teaching, I am also guided by Spirit, which, through each client's tree depiction, comes to me with remarkable accuracy.

There is only one person who I have never known to cry, and that is my second husband, for he is too much of an Arab man to cry. Many of our differences I now see were cultural, so I have had to remind myself what it is to be British and to live in this society and country rather than the one I left behind.

- 20 -

Discoveries

My learnings as a result of my story have been many, and I am not afraid to admit I have made some poor choices. Every decision and choice I have made, though, has had an outcome, and if that outcome has not been what I expected, I've chosen to take that as learning. I don't believe in mistakes. I believe in learning. Decisions and choices have outcomes that can be learnt from. For me, there is no such thing as a mistake.

At times, it has required me to examine who I am and my motivations deeply, though I have come to realise that these are in no way unique to me. I believe that every single one of us is searching for something and that we will make decisions along the way which may set us back a few steps.

Relationships

When it came to relationships, for example, I believed that I needed another person to complete me and make me happy. I married men I thought would do this, yet now I realise I was looking for someone to replace my absent father. The pain I felt did not come from his absence, though, that was deeper. The pain came from having a mother who believed her children to be a burden.

Many of us feel like we need others to complete us, to add to our personality and character, and somehow make us 'whole'. Having men in my life felt like the answer, yet in reality, there was never a problem.

Everything I needed was within me;
I just had to go through this journey to find it.

When we enter this world, we are separated from our essence, so we will never feel complete.

Taking Responsibility ~ Sympathy and Empathy

One of the most significant changes I have made within myself is taking responsibility for my actions and decisions rather than succumbing to the easier habit of blaming others. I used to blame my mother, for instance, for not loving me and for preventing me from attending university—yet that blame did nothing to change the situation. Instead, it simply gnawed away at me. We will not always agree with the decisions that others make, and we may not always appreciate the outcomes, though this is merely a part of human nature. We are all individuals, and we must possess the strength to believe in ourselves and extract the lessons from each setback it presents.

In essence, we are born alone and pass into the next world alone, so we need to take responsibility for our contribution to others' lives and look beyond the decisions we have felt wronged by. Part of being human is learning to sympathise and empathise—not only with others - we also need to learn to do this with ourselves. It is key that we understand the difference between the two.

We can *empathise* if we have experienced the same situation, and we will *sympathise* if we are merely bystanders to a situation and feel emotion for those involved.

With *empathy* comes a more profound understanding, a realisation that material things can only bring temporary happiness. The old saying, *'Money doesn't buy happiness,'* is true.

Yet, I know it's hard for those without money to believe this.

Money is the root of all evil - it doesn't need to be.

If we can only look inward and focus on ourselves, then we will find peace.

Peace of Mind

Permanent happiness comes from peace of mind, so we can ask ourselves: Is this decision going to give me peace of mind? Or is it going to disturb it? Is this person adding to my life or draining me emotionally?

It takes courage to truly do this, and I am aware of how easy it is for me to say this to you now that I have emerged on the other side. Yet it is precisely because I have reached that point that I can speak this truth. I know what it required for me to heal, and I understand what it takes for me to be happy. I had money, I had luxury, I had everything I thought I wanted—though in the end, it was never enough.

I firmly believe that if you learn the art of patience and tolerance, particularly towards others and their beliefs, then you can also gain insights from their experiences. In doing so, we can continue to coexist in a manner that supports one another rather than divides us.

My Spirit Guide

I want to end this section with thoughts from the wonderful John Hodge, who remains with me to this day. I believe that Earth is one of the few places where we, as Spiritual beings, can lead a human life – within the limitations of the human body. And, though it has limitations, we need our human body as a vehicle of expression. We need it to experience everything in the physical world – like some kind of contract we sign up to before moving onto our mortal existence. The lessons we learn form part of ***our book of life,*** and it is this ***book of life*** we need in order to meet our Spiritual destiny.

John Hodge gave me a simple explanation which I have never forgotten:

> *'Imagine a torch. The light we see from the torch is our soul. The body of the torch is our Spirit, and the hand that holds the torch is our God. The light of the soul on earth is an aspect of the soul that is encompassed within our Spirit.'*

Sometimes, we need to reach out to others – and that's okay. Those who have learned their own lessons can act as our guides as long as we open our minds and listen. It may be that we need to connect with someone who is closer to the Spiritual world, such as a medium or psychic, to get to where we need to be, and that's okay, too.

Though I know how hard it is for many to comprehend, I faithfully promise that my story has been guided by my Spiritual being and I know, without a shadow of a doubt, that it is this which has helped me in my darkest days.

- 21 -

The Next Chapter

We all have goals. During my twenties and thirties, I had several goals:

1. I wanted a four-bedroom detached house.
2. I wanted to own a luxury car.
3. I wanted to wear fashion labels.
4. I wanted to be viewed with respect.
5. I wanted money in the bank.
6. I wanted a husband.

And I achieved every single one of those goals – yet where did they leave me?

The thing about goals is that you achieve one which satiates you for a while, and then you want to move to the next goal and the next. *It is a never-ending chase of what we believe we should have or should achieve.* And because there is no such thing as 'perfection', we never get there.

Once I realised that, I revised my vision. In 2013, when my husband took his third wife, I understood that my time in the country was limited, so I decided to update my goals:

1. I wanted a house in the Lake District. Nothing big or fancy, just sufficient for Kitty and me.

And that was it. One goal. One material outcome if you like. The rest, I knew, would come from within.

It's not about these material goals; it's about who we want to be and who we want to become, and no amount of money will help us achieve that. For me, I prioritised things like:

- becoming a kinder person
- being more tolerant
- learning to forgive
- become more humanitarian
- learning to respond rather than react
- wanting to be remembered not for what I had achieved and what I did; instead wanting to be remembered for how I made/make people feel.

These goals are all about mastering the person within, the ego within, and putting this ego in its rightful place. It needs to sit **alongside** the heart, the mind, and the intuition, **not rule them**. Learning to master this ego has been one of my biggest journeys. Its mastery partly comes from learning to respond rather than react, though it's also about having a vision—a vision that is less about me and more about others.

My vision is to help as many people as possible move from their current state to their desired state. So often they are unhappy, and I want to help them find happiness.

I speak frequently about tolerance and patience, which go hand in hand, yet there appears to be little tolerance for others at times. People are marginalised based on their religions, beliefs, socioeconomic backgrounds, and ways of living – yet we are all human beings. In fact, we are all Spiritual beings occupying a human existence.

The definition of tolerance is the *'ability or willingness to tolerate the existence of opinions or behaviours that one dislikes or disagrees with, the capacity to endure continuous subjection to something such as drug or environmental conditions without adverse reactions'*, and it takes real strength to be tolerant of someone else's opinion.

So many people believe they are 'right' and anyone who disagrees is 'wrong'.

I was that person once upon a time.

I now see it for what it is: a lack of confidence.

If I expressed something and someone presented a stronger argument, that would indicate I was wrong. In the past, I was unwilling to be accepting of a differing opinion.

Patience is similar, too. I have always been a person who wants results—***now*** - sometimes, before I'd given my mind the opportunity to understand. This has resulted in me rushing into things and being quick to disagree. It didn't matter if the person disagreeing had done more work, more research, or more learning and was well-placed to challenge my decision; I didn't have the *tolerance* to accept anyone else's thoughts, input, or opinions.

Today, I realise that if I had allowed myself time to think (*patience*), there may have been a different and potentially more favourable outcome to some of my decisions.

Talking about favourable outcomes brings me back to **happiness** and what that looks like.

As we have already discussed, for some, *happiness* may be based on material possessions, while for others, it could be spending time with loved ones, for example. In reality, it doesn't matter what happiness looks like. What truly matters is that it is our happiness, and we are pursuing it for the right reasons. We are seeking to be happy for ourselves.

My vision is to support others in discovering their **happiness**, whether that will come from specific goals in their health and well-being journey or from the purchase of the latest gadget.

I will offer as much support and guidance as I can – and that's it. The new simple goal I have settled upon after the turmoil of the story I have shared.

I have a past and a vision for the future, both of which are linked by my capacity to learn from my own **book of life**. Now is the time for the next chapter.

My daughter is happy and settled. I am happy and settled.

I want to continue to turn my attention to helping others.

So, as we near the end of this book, I want to take a moment to acknowledge that we have finally uncovered the true reason for my writing it.

I want to help others - because if I can come out the other side and find happiness after all the ups and downs, then you absolutely can, too.

All you need is a little bit of guidance.

- 22 -

Exploring YOU

Now that you have heard my story, you might be ready to face some of your own challenges and ultimately see the possibilities for change. So how, in practical terms, can you make some simple yet powerful adjustments?

1. Counting to Twenty ~ Respond vs React

   The first tip I am going to share comes originally from my grandmother, who was forever reminding me to 'count to twenty'.

   Throughout the book, I have referred to *'responding'* rather than *'reacting'* to any given situation, primarily because *'responding'* usually achieves the most preferable outcome.

   Why? Because if we **react**, that usually happens instantly and we might not have considered the full implications of this reaction. If we take time to pause, our brains can run through various outcomes and choose the most appropriate ***response***.

   For my grandmother, the considered and most appropriate response always happened after a count of twenty:

   Counting 0 - 3: You're taking a couple of breaths here to create space between yourself and the situation/conversation.

Counting 4 - 8: Ask yourself questions such as: Is it my rational mind or my intuition that is responding? Is it short-term gain for long-term pain, or vice versa? Have I experienced this feeling/ reaction/situation before? If I have, am I using that for reference and remembering an unfavourable outcome?

Counting 9 - 13: Take a moment to tune into your true intuition, the one that arises from the centre of your forehead. Consider these four elements and listen to your intuition's response: (1) I like that person/situation (2) I dislike that person/situation (3) I'm uncertain about what to do/say (4) Am I able to let things simply unfold?

Counting 14: Remind yourself that we are Spiritual beings, and the reason we live human existences is to learn. It's fine when we experience pleasant emotions such as love, excitement, fondness, and protection. The challenge comes when we experience all the other emotions: betrayal, abandonment, depression, and so on. According to experts in the field of Emotional Intelligence (EQ), emotions are data, and like any data, they can be examined and the results determined.

Counting 15: Remember that it isn't always about us; sometimes, it's about others, too. That might mean embracing an outcome that we don't like. We are all teachers, both to teach and learn.

Counting 16: Remember that there is always a solution.

Counting 17: Take strength from your true intuition and be your authentic self. Look at the bigger picture.

Counting 18: The glass is always half full, not half empty. You don't have the capacity for negative thinking.

Counting 19: Be kind to yourself - remember you are loved, too.

Counting 20: Trust that you are being guided. You are never alone.

Now, take a deep breath and respond.

2. Letter Writing

   Letter writing is one of the most powerful tools that I use to help those (in particular) who may not be in a position to speak to or face the person they wish to address.

   If a client sitting in front of me is holding a great deal of anger and negative emotion toward a specific person, then I will ask them to put pen to paper and write a 'no-holds-barred' letter. This letter needs to be open, honest and frank, and there is only one caveat: if the person to whom the letter is addressed is still alive, IT MUST NEVER BE SENT. The intended recipient must NEVER READ THE LETTER.

   You might, for example, feel the need to explain to a parent the damage they caused you with their attitude or to an ex-partner about the emotional or physical abuse you suffered at their hands. As long as the letter never sees the light of day, it can be an incredibly powerful tool that allows us to offload and release emotions we have retained within.

   There is no right or wrong length for the letter; you simply write until you are done, and similarly, it has to be handwritten, not typed. The reason for this is that we engage far more neurons when we handwrite, which will increase the positive benefits of this exercise.

   Remember: this is not about avoiding responsibility or

having a difficult conversation, it is purely a mechanism to enable us to 'let go' of emotions that no longer serve us.

3. Gestalt Therapy Psychotherapy

> *"Gestalt therapy is a type of humanistic and person-centred therapy that focuses on the immediate here and now and how that can be explored to help you. It looks at how your past affects and influences how you're feeling in this moment rather than how you felt back then.[1]"*

One of the techniques from Gestalt Therapy that I have used to great effect is to ask the person who is struggling, to picture the individual who is causing them pain.

This works by placing a chair in the room and asking the client to imagine the person causing them pain sitting in it. As the chair is empty, this can sometimes be difficult to visualise, so if necessary, I'll place a photo of the relevant person on the chair.

I then encourage the client to speak to that person as if they were actually present. It can be uncomfortable at first; however, after a short time, the client is typically able to relax into it. We can then work backwards until we reach the point where the pain or suffering was inflicted, allowing the client to address their feelings directly with their tormentor. What is crucial here is for the client to express themselves freely; therefore, I provide a safe and supportive environment free from judgement. Expletives, if necessary, are acceptable!

The client may also become emotional, and that is fine, too. Whenever we or anyone we know is experiencing any type of emotion, it's useful to remember:

---

[1] https://www.bacp.co.uk/about-therapy/types-of-therapy/gestalt/

- » Emotions are thoughts.
- » Thoughts are living things.
- » Living things use energy.
- » Energy has a mass.

An emotion is a thought, which is a living entity that consumes energy. Consuming energy depletes our resources; therefore, it follows that emotions drain our energy, meaning they wear us down. If we can release emotions, thoughts, and beliefs—especially those we may have held for many years—this can be healing and profoundly cathartic.

You can try this technique at home, though I would always recommend practising it in the company of a trained professional who can support you with any outcomes and/or discoveries that may arise.

4. <u>Stop, Start, Continue</u>

To begin trying this technique, first consider something that you want to STOP, for example, smoking, overeating, negative thinking, etc.

Then, identify what you need to START doing to enable you to stop the behaviour or habit that you have identified. So, if you want to stop overeating, for example, you might start swimming as a form of exercise instead. Or, if you are constantly experiencing negative thoughts and wish to stop those, then perhaps you will consciously start to think of every glass as half-full rather than half-empty.

Let's consider chocolate for a moment. Ask yourself: Do I really *need* this chocolate bar, or do I merely *want* it? If the answer indicates that you *want* it rather than *need* it, then move on and replace it with a glass of water. If you believe you *need* the chocolate bar, ask yourself *why*. What is it going to provide you? Are you eating out of habit or loneliness? Will consuming the chocolate bar change that? Challenging ourselves in this way helps us uncover the reason behind the behaviour, allowing us to understand the root cause and begin to implement a lasting change.

Once you have started to make the change, then you need to CONTINUE with the new behaviour to build a habit. When the new behaviour becomes a habit, you will have successfully 'stopped' the original behaviour and issue.

A great way to begin your STOP, START, CONTINUE process is to write those three words on the top of a piece of paper. Then, think about your behaviours or habits that you wish to address and list these beneath the relevant word. For example:

STOP	START	CONTINUE
Smoking	Exercising	Healthy Eating

It doesn't matter how many are in each column. The point of this is to provide a framework so that you can identify which areas of your life you'd like to focus on.

5. Where Does It All Begin?

Note: I will be introducing some beliefs here that may not align with your own. As you read this section, I encourage you to remain open-minded, but I also suggest that you take only what you perceive as beneficial and/or comfortable from it.

As I have alluded to before, I believe that we are already Spiritual beings who are living a human existence before entering the physical plane.

This might sound a bit confusing, so I will simplify it by looking more closely at why I believe we inhabit a human existence:

» Before we exist in human form, our Spiritual self will agree on the lessons we will learn and teach whilst living as humans.
» When born into our physical body, we will have no recollection of this agreement or these lessons.
» Our memories are not usually reliable until we are preschool age (5 years old). Whilst we cannot remember, we will have already learned some of our (agreed) lessons from the right people, such as our parents.
» The people we encounter throughout our lives are then deliberately placed so that we can access the right Spiritual lessons at the right time.
» We must also contend with our ego, which not only wants to be heard, it is often ***not*** our friend. It is frequently our ego that causes conflict with others, including those who are our Spiritual teachers.
» If we extrapolate this, we might consider a neighbour who consistently parks in front of our driveway as an example. This will lead to a lack of harmony and diminished tolerance towards our neighbour.
» If we work on building our tolerance, we can become more understanding of this neighbour. This gets even easier if we remember that, ultimately, it is our neighbour's ego that wishes to be heard. Sometimes, others can set their ego aside and meet us halfway, yet there are occasions when they are unable to do so. In that situation, as long as we can keep our ego in check, we will be in a much better position to maintain peace and harmony.

> When we talk about our time as a physical body, it is impossible for anyone to tell us when it will end. I believe that we are here in our physical form until we have learned the lessons we agreed to—the contract with our Creator if you like. Once we have learned these lessons, it is time for us to return to the world of Spirit.

Here's the argument *against* the above, though:

If all of this is true, why do bad things happen?

In truth, there is no definitive answer to this question. It is my personal belief that behind every event or occurrence lies a lesson we are destined to learn. Sometimes, when we are experiencing traumatic times, it can be helpful to believe that 'everything happens for a reason,' which is something I often hear. Though we can neither prove nor disprove this, we can use this belief as a support and coping mechanism to help us through the toughest times.

We can also think about what happened before or after the (bad) event. Did we, for example, do something differently that day? Did we make a new acquaintance? Did we bump into someone we hadn't seen for a long time? While this won't help us understand why the 'bad' thing occurred immediately, it will assist us in identifying a pattern of behaviour, habits, thoughts, or actions which might lead us to the lesson we are meant to learn from that particular event.

One thing I am absolutely clear about is that people enter our lives to teach us lessons, and whether someone is in our life temporarily or becomes a lifelong partner, they have been placed there by the world of Spirit. The world of Spirit is, therefore, continually manoeuvring us, shifting our perspective and providing us with signs that lead us to our next lesson, urging us to meet the people we need to in order to develop and grow.

*"People come into your life for a reason,
a season or a lifetime
When you figure out which one it is,
you will know what to do for each person "*

~ Brian A. "Drew" Chalker

- 23 -

Final Insights and Wisdom

Over the years, I have come to realise that regardless of any other socio-economic or financial factors, every single person I have ever helped has wanted only two things:

1. They want to reduce any suffering or avoid it altogether.
2. They want to be happy.

With that in mind, I would like to share some of the insights I have gained.

Everyone who comes to me wants to move away from where they are. They want inner peace and happiness. Happiness and peace mean different things to different people; for some, it might be a Ferrari on the drive, whereas for others, it might be access to fresh running water. Often, though, there is a common theme that can link the place where we find ourselves to the place where we would like to exist.

The most common issues I encounter are:
- marriage issues
- weight gain
- negative habits such as smoking
- depression and anxiety
- addictive behaviours and drug use
- abuse
- relationship issues
- negative thinking
- living in the past, not the present or even the future
- a lack of confidence

Marriage Issues

If we consider marriage issues as a starting point, we can break them down in a way that may be more beneficial for both parties. Let's say John met Jane when they were 22 and 19 years old, respectively. After a few years, John and Jane marry and go on to have children.

As a result of giving birth, Jane's body changes, her outlook changes, and her priorities change - yet the same might not be said for John.

When John and Jane come to see me, they are in their forties. John struggles because he wants Jane to be the same woman she was when they first married. However, she isn't because a lot has changed. She is still the same Jane deep down, though on the surface, her priorities and interests have changed.

When John and Jane first met, they were remarkably compatible, and it didn't take long for them to commit to one another for life. This is not to say they thought the other was perfect – far from it – they were able though, to embrace their differences and overcome any issues which threatened to derail their relationship.

Today, with many years behind them and the addition of children, the pressure on each is much greater. The differences, which in the early days seemed minuscule, are now becoming more apparent and harder to ignore. What they end up with are two entirely different lists of expectations from each other and their marriage. With these divisive lists, John and Jane are now trying to maintain a relationship from two very different perspectives—the equivalent of pushing water uphill.

The key is to go back to the beginning, to ask John and Jane why they got together, what they loved about each other, and what their hopes and dreams were.

Sometimes, I find that men, in particular, find it hard to be second in their wives' affection once the children come along. This can be an unsaid source of tension, which, if allowed to fester, will lead to heartache in later years.

If, however, John and Jane can rediscover what they loved about each other and realise that their love still endures, then there is every chance that, with hard work and, crucially, communication, their marriage can withstand the inevitable bumps in the road.

Yes, our closest relationships are all about the expectations we place on each other, though what is often forgotten is that they are also about responsibility. The responsibility to ourselves and each other. Let's expand on this a little.

Personal Responsibility

Take a moment to reflect on your school days or formative years, considering the events for which you attributed blame to your parents or teachers. With the advantage of time and reflection, can you truly say that you were justified in placing the blame on them?

Often, the answer here is no.

I have realised that humans find it challenging to learn to take personal responsibility and accept the outcomes of our decisions. We want to avoid making mistakes, yet what if there was no such thing as a mistake? What if every mistake was simply a learning opportunity?

If we consider our situation in this way, we can acknowledge that while others may have guided us, we have ultimately made the decision.

Imagine a scenario in which you **take all of the learnings and wisdom with you into the next situation** rather than the **emotions of the experience** itself.

Part of the future is often written in the past, and nothing is more indicative of this than those who are struggling with issues related to their weight.

Weight Struggles

When we are first born, we have no control over anything. We are fed, changed, bathed, and put to bed according to others in our lives. As we get older we develop independence and are able to make some of our own decisions, the big one being what we are going to eat and when.

Initially, we aim to assert our authority over ourselves by making choices about what we eat, believing we are in control. However, at some point, we may lose that control and struggle to find our way back. If our control over our eating habits falters, it can easily lead to weight gain.

I start by working out why or what caused the loss of control. The easiest way to do that is to find a time when we last remember being completely happy with no issues or concerns about weight.

Once we have found this time, then we can dig deeper and look into events, thoughts, feelings and behaviours that may have occurred around that time which might have caused us to use food as an 'escape'.

From this, we can often deduce the root cause, which is **not** a loss or lack of control; overeating is symptomatic of the unhappiness and suffering from which we are trying to escape.

In the same way as we stripped back the relationship between John and Jane, we can strip back our relationship with food. Then, if we can identify what we are replacing with food, we can better find the right emotional support or solution.

It's precisely the same with money - because it honestly can't buy happiness. Just because you can have whatever you want, it doesn't mean that deep down, you are happy. Sometimes, incredibly rich people admit they would be a lot happier if they didn't have money.

It's All Really Simple

In all of these situations, it comes right back to the two basic premises I mentioned earlier:

1. we want to avoid suffering
2. we want to be happy

If we can learn to take a **step back**, **respond** rather than **react**, become **more tolerant** and **understanding**, and be **kind** to ourselves, I firmly believe that we will be following not only our Spiritual path, we will also be on the path to a life of true fulfilment, peace, and happiness.

About the Author

With over 30 years experience incorporating NLP, mindfulness, EQ, stress management and healing into her practice, Debbie Amal has pretty much seen it all.

Through her own painful journey she has developed methodologies which help her clients to gain a deeper understanding of their life's purpose.

Debbie Amal began her career in the corporate world where she achieved great success. She accumulated every material object and met every single goal whilst living a comfortable and envied existence. Through her first marriage Debbie Amal was blessed with her daughter, Kitty, and reached a point where she believed her life was complete. Until one day she realised that it wasn't.

Though Debbie Amal knew she had a psychic gift from an early age, it wasn't until her first marriage hit the rocks that she began to really draw guidance and comfort from the Spirit world. What unfolded in the subsequent years as she both followed and ignored her intuition, was a life blighted by pain. From this pain came true and rich learning and now Debbie Amal has found her true place and purpose. It is from this place she writes.

Debbie Amal now spends her days working with those who are physically drained, emotionally and mentally lost, confused or at a crisis point in their lives as well as those who are out of control, unhappy or on a spiritual path they are unsure of. From her time in the corporate world, Debbie Amal has come to learn it is a place where the ego rules and the heart is hidden so now, using her experience, qualifications and above all, her intuitive connection to Spirit, she aims to reduce ego and increase heart space. Debbie Amal states that she 'loves what she does' which shows in her 'passion, kindness and compassion' for everyone she sees.

> *"People travel to all four corners of the earth and yet the greatest journey that they face, lies in journeying within."*
>
> *~ Debbie Amal Loring*

Debbie Amal can be found at www.yugenwisdom.com

www.ingramcontent.com/pod-product-compliance
Lightning Source LLC
Chambersburg PA
CBHW052050070526
44584CB00017B/2115